What Your Colleagues Are Saying

MW00998104

Colleen offers literacy teachers a valuable comprehension instruction "hack": help students get inside the brains of the writers they read by doing the same kind of writing themselves *before* they read. She argues convincingly that the more students understand how something was made, the better they'll understand it when they encounter it as readers. She doesn't just offer compelling research to prove it; she offers teachers dozens of paired lessons so that students will read and write information texts with more power. The lessons are streamlined to allow students maximum time for practice and application, and to help the busy teacher go from the page to the classroom quickly and almost effortlessly. I encourage all upper elementary and middle school teachers to give these lesson sets a try!

—Jen Serravallo, author of *The Reading Strategies Book* and *The Writing Strategies Book*

Most professional books on teaching nonfiction focus on teaching writing or reading, but not both. In this unique book, Colleen Cruz shows us how to teach complementary writing and reading lessons that will help students use what they're learning about nonfiction writing to help them become more powerful nonfiction readers.

—Carl Anderson, author of *How's It Going?* and *The Teacher's Guide to Writing Conferences*

This book refuels your energy to think about the way you plan and teach reading and writing. Colleen holds strong to the tenets of workshop—choice, voice, and agency—then beautifully blends the lessons and theory with her vast experience in classrooms, new research on writing and reading, and the dance we do with it all now in the digital world. The structure of the book and the lessons are completely accessible for all teachers, the way Colleen believes the learning and craft to be accessible for all students. It's a game-changer for those looking to augment and reflect on their current workshop model and for those who are going to give it a go. Colleen is with you every step of the way.

—Sara K. Ahmed, author, speaker, and literacy coach at NIST International School, Bangkok, Thailand

For Kathleen, my first true reading teacher. Your belief in the power of literacy, and the power it gives children and their teachers, seeps through every pore of this book. You are missed.

Writers Read Better: Nonfiction

50+ PAIRED LESSONS THAT TURN WRITING CRAFT WORK INTO POWERFUL GENRE READING

M. Colleen Cruz

FOR INFORMATION:

Corwin

A SAGE Company

2455 Teller Road

Thousand Oaks, California 91320

(800) 233-9936

www.corwin.com

SAGE Publications Ltd.

1 Oliver's Yard

55 City Road

London EC1Y 1SP

United Kingdom

SAGE Publications India Pvt. Ltd.

B 1/I 1 Mohan Cooperative Industrial Area

Mathura Road, New Delhi 110 044

India

SAGE Publications Asia-Pacific Pte. Ltd.

3 Church Street

#10-04 Samsung Hub

Singapore 049483

Director and Publisher, Corwin Classroom: Lisa Luedeke

Acquisitions Editors: Wendy Murray and Tori Bachman

Editorial Development Manager: Julie Nemer

Senior Editorial Assistant: Sharon Wu

Production Editors: Amy Schroller and Laureen Gleason

Copy Editor: Jared Leighton

Typesetter: C&M Digitals (P) Ltd.

Proofreader: Susan Schon

Indexer: Jeanne Busemeyer

Cover Designer: Gail Buschman

Marketing Manager: Brian Grimm

Printed in the United States of America.

Library of Congress Cataloging-in-Publication Data
Names: Cruz, Colleen, author.
Title: Writers read better : nonfiction : 50+ paired lessons that turn writing craft work into powerful genre reading / Colleen Cruz.
Description: Thousand Oaks, California : Corwin, [2018] | Includes bibliographical references and index.
Identifiers: LCCN 2018012836 | ISBN 9781506311234 (pbk. : alk. paper)
Subjects: LCSH: Language arts (Secondary) | English language—Composition and exercises—Study and teaching (Secondary) | Reading (Secondary)
Classification: LCC LB1631 .C78 2018 | DDC 428.0071/2—dc23
LC record available at https://lccn.loc.gov/2018012836

This book is printed on acid-free paper.

Certified Chain of Custody
SUSTAINABLE FORESTRY INITIATIVE
Promoting Sustainable Forestry
www.sfiprogram.org
SFI-01268
SFI label applies to text stock

18 19 20 21 22 10 9 8 7 6 5 4 3 2 1

CONTENTS

PART 3

Visit the companion website at **resources.corwin.com/
writersreadbetter** for videos and downloadable resources.

LIST OF VIDEOS

Note from the Publisher: The author has provided video and web content in this book that is available to you through QR codes. To read a QR code, you must have a smartphone or a tablet with a camera. We recommend that you download a QR code reader app that is made specifically for your phone or tablet brand.

Videos may also be accessed at **resources.corwin.com/writersreadbetter**

Video 1

Lesson 6: Writing: *Using Structure to Convey the Writer's Intent*

In this video, I model this lesson with one of the pilot classes. I show how, as writers, the students might consider ways to structure their writing purposefully.

Video 2

Lesson 6: Reading: *Inferring the Author's Intent by Noticing Structure*

In this video, I model this lesson with the same class. I make the connection between what the students learned previously about crafting purposeful structures and how they can also identify these same structures in the informational texts they might read.

Video 3

Lesson 8: Writing: *Structure Within Sections: Stacking Information*

I chose to film this lesson because most pilot teachers said that once they'd seen me demonstrate it, they "got it" easily. It is a lesson that sounds much more complicated on paper than it is in practice!

Video 4

This lesson is the sister lesson to the writing lesson, giving students an opportunity to use the same manipulatives they used in their writing work in their reading. This is one of those lessons that feels especially powerful when taught after its writing component.

Solutions at a Glance

If you want to address this common reading challenge . . .	First, teach this writing lesson . . .	Then, this paired reading lesson
Literal comprehension of details	• Lesson 9: Drafting With Placeholders for Later Facts • Lesson 10: Taking a Draft Break to Research	• Lesson 9: Using Jots to Note Facts Quickly • Lesson 10: Noticing the Various Ways Authors Use Quotation Marks
Importance of information	• Lesson 15: Reordering Information With Intention • Lesson 16: Exploring How Writers Weight Information to Signal Import	• Lesson 15: Noticing the Effect of Information's Placement • Lesson 16: Looking at Texts to See How Volume Can Signify Importance
Main idea	• Lesson 18: Connections and Disconnections Across Paragraphs and Pages • Lesson 21: First and Last Words: Intros and Conclusions That Attract and Linger • Lesson 24: Creating Strong Titles and Subtitles	• Lesson 18: Tracing Connections and Disconnections in Transitions • Lesson 21: Studying an Author's First and Last Words • Lesson 24: Titles and Subtitles That Convey Meaning
Text structure	• Lesson 4: Narrowing Down a Broad Topic • Lesson 5: The Role of Structure in Informational Texts • Lesson 6: Using Structure to Convey the Writer's Intent • Lesson 8: Structure Within Sections: Stacking Information • Lesson 25: The Many Purposes of Paragraphs	• Lesson 4: Understanding Topics and Subtopics • Lesson 5: Considering How Choices in Structure Affect Meaning • Lesson 6: Inferring the Author's Intent by Noticing Structure • Lesson 8: Identifying the Way Information Is Stacked • Lesson 25: Seeing Paragraphs as an Author's Organizational Tool
Text features	• Part 3 Digital Writing Lesson: Adding Dimensions to Writing Through Multimodal Features • Lesson 23: Creating Text Features to Enhance and Add Information	• Part 3 Digital Reading Lesson: Multimodal Readers Prioritize Synthesis • Lesson 23: Integrating Text Features Within and Across Texts
Background knowledge	• Lesson 2: Write About What You Take for Granted • Lesson 9: Drafting With Placeholders for Later Facts • Lesson 10: Taking a Draft Break to Research	• Lesson 2: Learning Unexpected Things From Familiar Topics • Lesson 9: Using Jots to Note Facts Quickly • Lesson 10: Noticing the Various Ways Authors Use Quotation Marks
Vocabulary	• Lesson 19: Vocabulary's Starring Role in Informational Texts • Lesson 27: Using Meaning to Make Smart Spelling Decisions	• Lesson 19: Expecting and Responding to the Subject's Vocabulary • Lesson 27: The Role of Etymology for Readers

If you want to address this common reading challenge . . .	First, teach this writing lesson . . .	Then, this paired reading lesson
Author's purpose	<ul><li>Lesson 1: An Author's Expertise Matters</li><li>Lesson 3: The Relationship Between an Author's Passions and Stance</li><li>Lesson 6: Using Structure to Convey the Writer's Intent</li><li>Part 1 Digital Writing Lesson: Choosing the Best Platform for Your Information and Audience</li><li>Lesson 7: Drafting What You're Most Ready to Write</li><li>Lesson 11: Drafting With an Audience in Mind</li><li>Lesson 13: Drafting to Someone Else's Specifications</li></ul>	<ul><li>Lesson 1: Considering the Source</li><li>Lesson 3: Identifying an Author's Stance</li><li>Lesson 6: Inferring the Author's Intent by Noticing Structure</li><li>Part 1 Digital Reading Lesson: Considering Why Authors Might Choose Analogue or Digital Mediums</li><li>Lesson 7: Spotting What's Most Important to an Author</li><li>Lesson 11: Noticing the Different Genres of Various Publications on the Same Topic</li><li>Lesson 13: Noticing a Publisher's Approach</li></ul>
Critical thinking	<ul><li>Part 2 Digital Writing Lesson: Fact-Checking Digital Information for Accuracy</li><li>Lesson 14: Deciding What's Most Important to Revise</li><li>Lesson 20: The Slipperiness of Facts</li><li>Lesson 22: Choosing When to Quote, Describe, or Summarize</li><li>Lesson 28: Making Publishing Decisions Based on the Intended Audience</li></ul>	<ul><li>Part 2 Digital Reading Lesson: Identifying False Information</li><li>Lesson 14: Identifying and Questioning the Author's Values</li><li>Lesson 20: Reading With Eyes Wide Open for Bias</li><li>Lesson 22: Identifying Sources and Considering Their Reliability</li><li>Lesson 28: Judging the Effectiveness of an Author's Decisions</li></ul>
Strategy flexibility	<ul><li>Lesson 17: The Power of Story</li><li>Lesson 22: Choosing When to Quote, Describe, or Summarize</li></ul>	<ul><li>Lesson 17: Switching Strategies When Authors Use Story in Expository Text</li><li>Lesson 22: Identifying Sources and Considering Their Reliability</li></ul>
Tone and mood	<ul><li>Lesson 12: Drafting in a Mood or Tone That Matches the Content</li><li>Lesson 26: Punctuating With Intention</li></ul>	<ul><li>Lesson 12: Noticing When the Tone Doesn't Match the Topic</li><li>Lesson 26: Looking Across Texts With an Eye to Punctuation</li></ul>
Response to texts	<ul><li>Lesson 9: Drafting With Placeholders for Later Facts</li><li>Part 4 Digital Writing: Opening and Maintaining a Conversation With Audiences</li></ul>	<ul><li>Lesson 9: Using Jots to Note Facts Quickly</li><li>Part 4 Digital Reading: Responding Digitally to the Text to Deepen Understanding</li></ul>

 Available for download at **resources.corwin.com/writersreadbetter**

ACKNOWLEDGMENTS

As with all books, there is a multitude of people, too numerous to count, who helped bring this book into the world.

First and foremost, I must thank my mentor and friend, Lucy Calkins, who not only is one of my biggest influences and teachers in all things literacy but also is the person who nudged me to agree to this series and whose idea it was to make information writing the first book in the series.

I also need to thank the entire Reading and Writing Project Community. Thank you for encouraging me through this book, being a bouncing board for my craziest ideas, and your all-around brilliance. I'd like to especially thank Brooke Gellar for her steady supply of cookies; Shana Frazin for her critical eye and book recommendations; and Janet Steinberg, who was the first person who suggested I turn my idea of teaching writing before reading into a book . . . and who kept nagging me until I did.

I'd also like to thank my dear friends and colleagues whose influence and support for this series will be evident to anyone familiar with their work. Thank you Jennifer Serravallo for introducing me to Lisa Luedeke and helping me think through the series as a whole. Thank you Carl Anderson for helping me to see where this book and series belong in the world. Thank you Kate Roberts for believing me into this project. Thank you Maggie Roberts for making me laugh and see the absurdity when the going got tough.

I need to thank all of the teachers and colleagues who experimented with this work from its earliest stages onward: P.S. 295, P.S. 116, P.S. 176, and especially the two main pilot teachers, Connie Pertuz-Mesa and Kerri Hook. This book would not be as authentic, as practical, or as filled with student work and pictures if it weren't for you.

The acknowledgments wouldn't be complete without thanking my biggest cheerleaders, the Wednesday Night Writing Group: Barbara, Kristin, Connie, Sarah, Kerri, and Australia.

I also want to thank the entire Corwin team, particularly Lisa Luedeke, who was a thoughtful and patient editor, even as we both dealt with the most amazing life ups and downs over the course of its writing. I'd also like to thank Wendy Murray, who helped usher the book through its middle stages.

Then, a huge debt of gratitude is owed to my superhero editor who came in to put this book to bed and held my hand until the end, Tori Bachman. And, of course, Amy Schroller and Laureen Gleason, production editors, who ensured that this book is as lovely as it is.

Finally, I am especially indebted to my family. My two sons, Sam and Nico, were very patient through the whole writing process, even if they were slightly disappointed in the fact that my book wasn't a "real" picture book. My long-book-suffering partner, Nadine, has helped birth almost ten books in our almost twenty years together. Her encouragement and willingness to take up my slack made it possible for me to finish this book. Her talent and skill as a photographer and filmmaker made it possible to bring its pages to life.

INTRODUCTION

A couple of years ago, I was sitting around with some friends. Some of them were writers; some of them weren't. One of us had a newspaper out.

"Let's play a game," I said. "I read the headline, and you guess how the lead is going to go. Extra points if you manage to guess how the whole article will go."

The headlines looked something like this:

- Refugees Struggle to Find Safety

- Teachers Stressed, Overworked, and Underpaid

- Can *Anyone* Afford Their Dream Home?

- Hero Canine Saves Toddler

- Stocks Disappoint

My friends were intrigued, so I started. I scrolled through all of the sections: sports, features, news, and opinion. And each headline I read aloud led to sure-footed predictions as to how the article would likely unfold.

Here's what I found interesting and what has served as the spark of this book: the friends who were writers for a living—in particular, the ones who wrote nonfiction—were significantly better at the game. Just based on the headlines, they were able to guess if the lead paragraph was more likely an anecdote, a description, a statement of fact, even a question. My nonwriter friends, on the other hand, had about the same odds as playing the slots. Sure, they guessed right some of the time, but most of the time they did not.

This got me to thinking about other places in my life where writers had a direct advantage over nonwriters when it came to reading. I could point to many times in my life when I was able to make a prediction, develop an inference, or make a deep interpretation more easily, quickly, and precisely than other people. And it's not because I'm some sort of clairvoyant. It's because I am a writer of many genres, which means I have experience with crafting texts: knowing how they are made from the inside.

Many years ago, Katie Ray taught me that we can—and should—show kids how to read like writers. In her seminal book, *Wondrous Words* (1999), she teaches us to let children know that writers read differently. This is because as writers we learn how to write from modeling our work off other writers. When writers read a beautiful sentence, we don't just ooh and ah. We also study it. How many commas? What parts of speech? How does it fit with the sentences around it? Writers do this so that we can apply the style and technique to our own writing and elevate it. Since that book's publication, several other books have come out that have developed and furthered Ray's ideas, including *Writers Are Readers* by Lester Laminack and Reba Wadsworth. This book, along with the other two books in this *Writers Read Better* series, posits that there is another part of this equation, another spring to be tapped. *When writers of all ages write a lot, they become better readers because they have the inside scoop on the work writers do.*

For instance, students who are immersed in a writing workshop might spend weeks writing one piece in a particular genre. This work could make them uniquely equipped to read examples of those texts with ease and deep understanding.

As another example, I have no doubt that Malcolm Gladwell, author of such renowned informational books as *The Tipping Point* (2000) and *Blink* (2005), is a highly attuned and skilled reader of informational texts. In fact, he is likely a stronger reader of this type of work than a writer who specializes in another genre. It is easy to imagine Gladwell sitting in his reading chair poring over a book, anticipating before he turns a page how this next section will go or synthesizing the author's message with ease because he recognizes some of the author's moves as ones he has made himself.

Of course, theories such as this are worthless if they do not apply to real kids. So not too long after my experiment in newspaper prediction, I tried it with a class of third-grade students who were smack dab in the middle of a unit on nonfiction reading. I sat next to a student who told me about her nonfiction book. Mainly, she focused on the cool facts she was learning and pointed out the ickiest pictures. While I was pleased with her engagement, I wondered about other work she could be doing as a reader.

I said, "Hey, can you tell me a bit about the structure of the book you're reading?"

She looked at me with one eyebrow raised. "What?"

"You know, the structure of your book. How it's organized and how the various parts fit together."

She blinked at me.

I looked around the classroom for charts that might refer to the task of considering structure as readers. I didn't spot any reading charts right away, but I did see some writing charts—charts that reminded me that this was a girl who was nearing the end of her unit on writing informational books. All at once, I had an idea.

"Can you grab your writing folder?"

She shrugged her shoulders and pulled it out of her desk.

I said, "Take out your informational book—the one you've been writing."

When she did, I said, "Can you tell me a bit about the structure of *your* book? For instance, could you turn to the table of contents and walk me through how you decided to structure your writing?"

She smiled, delighted for the opportunity to share her hard work and expertise. She took me through her decisions, pointing out where she talked about parts of her topic, where she wrote in sequence, and even the part where she experimented with a little question-and-answer structure.

I continued by asking, "Now, can you set the book you wrote next to the book you're reading? And can you tell me about the book you're reading? Tell me about the ways your author structured his piece that are similar to the choices you made and places where the decisions were different."

This time there was no silence. As if by magic, the child who had just waggled an eyebrow at me shared several details about the structural choices the author made.

This series is designed to capitalize on that magic. But just like the famous magicians Penn & Teller have made a career of demystifying magic, showing the audience how the tricks *really* work, so too will this book demystify the connection between reading and writing. Specifically, I will show you clear and explicit ways to build off the reciprocity between reading and writing. I will teach you how to take the work that your students do in their writing and repurpose it in order to offer them a lever of understanding into challenging reading tasks.

No matter how you teach, whatever your curriculum is, or how much time you have, you will find something in this book that will not only help bring more energy and connectivity to your literacy instruction but also maximize your time and your students' ability to transfer literacy skills.

In "How to Use This Book," which begins on page xx, I go into the nitty-gritty details about the long-term academic and field research this book is built upon. I give specific explanations for why the book is organized the way it is and tips for how to best utilize it while staying true to your own literacy instruction needs and goals.

When first crafting this series, I relied on my own experience as a classroom teacher and as a consultant for the Teachers College Reading and Writing Project, who has had the honor of working with thousands of teachers. I also considered the fact that all teachers have a unique set of circumstances and students whom they will teach. Ultimately, I wanted to highlight the powerful role of excellent writing instruction in developing students as writers as well as readers—and to make this book as user-friendly, accessible, and flexible as it could possibly be.

HOW TO USE THIS BOOK

When laying out the idea for this book, I knew that there were many fantastic educators who had walked this road before me. As I designed the lessons, I was mindful of the fact that teachers who would pick up this book might very well have a curriculum already in place for informational reading and writing. For example, folks who use Lucy Calkins's and the Reading and Writing Project's *Units of Study for Writing* or *Units of Study for Reading* series (full disclosure, I coauthored four units in the series) were likely to be following those lessons very closely. Other teachers might have several excellent support materials such as *Nonfiction Craft Lessons* by JoAnn Portalupi and Ralph Fletcher (2001). Still others might have a basal reading program or use a curriculum they wrote. No matter what the case may be, the lessons from this book can be easily incorporated into your literacy teaching.

As I mentioned earlier, the reading and writing lessons are simpatico, but perhaps the most unusual feature of this book is that the writing lessons are designed for you to teach them before you teach the paired reading lesson. In fact, my main purpose for writing this book is that I believe that some of the toughest-to-teach skills in reading are best approached by teaching them in writing first. You might say the writing lessons set up a "slam dunk" in the paired reading lesson, like basketball players provide assists. So when teaching literacy, know that the lessons for both reading and writing were conceived together to make it easier for you to bring that coherence into your classroom. One wise way to use this book—and the other books in this series—is to identify reading skills your students need additional instruction in, whether whole class or small group, and then go about teaching their writing counterparts first, before looping back and trying the paired reading lesson.

In addition, I really want you to make the lessons in this book your own: from the order you teach them in to the specific examples you use. In order to support this customization, I purposefully highlight in blue parts of each lesson that you could easily replace with your own content, either because you have a topic that is especially exciting to your students or because you need more or less challenging texts. That way, while planning, you can quickly scan those parts of the lesson and decide if they need to be replaced with your own material or if what I have used will work for you and your students.

You will also notice that I use the terms *information* and *nonfiction* interchangeably throughout the book, even though that is not precisely correct. This is because many teachers and schools use these terms interchangeably. For the record, I tend to see information writing and reading as any type of text whose primary job is to inform its readers about a particular topic. This writing tends to be expository in nature, with the organizing structure centered on the topic. Most of the lessons in this book assume that this is the type of reading and writing your students are engaged in. I tend to see *nonfiction* as a term that casts a wider net and encompasses a variety of different structures and genres, from expository all-about books to biographies to nonfiction poems to informative lectures, such as TED Talks, to lots of different things in between.

I see readers using this book in one of three main ways:

1. **Pick and choose lessons to complement your current nonfiction lessons or string a few together to create a small detour within a current unit, based on what you know your students need**. This should be fairly simple, since the majority of the lessons in this book, particularly those that focus on readers learning from their writing work, are unique and thus are not likely to be lessons that you have already planned to teach. This is especially true when considering teaching writing in support of reading and not the other way around.

2. **Use the lessons only for conferences and small-group work**. Because these lessons are fairly different than other curriculum, you are unlikely to have redundancy even if you are a service provider or an interventionist. However, the skills taught in this book are skills that will strengthen any reader and writer.

3. **Teach most of the lessons, in order**. It can be used as a complete curriculum for teaching the writing and reading of informational texts and will align with most state, national, and international literacy standards. You can alter and add as you see fit.

No matter how you decide to use this book, I recommend that you work within the framework of frequently teaching a writing lesson *first*, as a scaffold for a reading lesson. However, it does not matter whether you choose to teach your reading and writing units concurrently, teach the writing unit first, or stagger the writing unit a few sessions or weeks ahead of the reading work.

This approach might feel strange at first. Many of us, myself included, are used to teaching reading first, organizing our reading instruction and curriculum to help improve student writing. And thanks to the brilliant work of Katie Wood Ray's *Wondrous Words* (1999), many of us came to understand the incredible power and opportunity afforded by studying mentor texts in reading in order to borrow craft, structure, and other writing moves from published writers. This is still fundamental and important work for teachers and young writers to engage in. I would be hard pressed to imagine an engaging and productive writing classroom that does not lean on the work the students have already done during reading instruction.

The Writers Read Better series builds off a body of research that suggests writing instruction and writing process may be the "alpha dog" after all; in fact, it may be better suited than reading to help learners develop craft and comprehension holistically. Research shows that not only are reading and writing inextricably connected, but also, the teaching of writing—and specifically, the linking of writing skills to reading work—is a powerful move for deepening comprehension (Burns, Roe, & Ross, 1992; Calkins, 1983; Chew, 1985; Gentry & Peha, 2013; Graham & Hebert, 2010; Hornsby, Sukarna, & Parry, 1988). Furthermore, teachers who have piloted the work in this book have reported that by flipping the order of instruction to begin with writing before the connected reading lesson, and then explicitly making those connections for students, teachers have greatly enhanced the students' depth as well as speed of understanding. This has proved to be especially the case for students who initially found the reading skills being practiced to be particularly challenging, obtuse, or abstract.

Key Components of the Reading and Writing Workshop

The basic ideas and philosophical underpinnings of the work in this book are based on the reading and writing workshop model. I am a long-time member of the Teachers College Reading and Writing Project Community and serve there as the Director of Innovation. It is the educational community where I grew up as an educator, and much of the thinking and my personal interpretation of the workshop model comes from that community's influence, which leans on the work of such esteemed educators and researchers as Donald Graves, Donald Murray, Lucy Calkins, Marie Clay, Irene Fountas, Gay Sue Pinnell, Stephanie Harvey, Nancie Atwell, and Richard Allington, to name a few.

You do not need to have a reading or writing workshop in your classroom to teach the lessons from this book. However, the following section highlights the key components of the workshop model that are assumed in the lesson write-ups.

The Workshop Model Structure

Most days a workshop session, whether it is reading or writing, include the following elements.

1. A short lesson, approximately seven to fifteen minutes in length, in which the teacher teaches a strategy that the students might use during their work time.

2. Independent work time, which takes from twenty to forty minutes. Students work independently, in partnerships, or in small groups. During the independent work time, the teacher also works with some of the students in conferences or small groups to support and guide as needed.

If you do not currently teach using the workshop model, note that it involves less whole-class instruction from the front of the room and much more teaching to small groups and individuals. Consequently, the lessons in this book are designed to be short to allow students maximum amounts of time to practice their reading and writing skills.

The Importance of Choice

In the typical workshop classroom, students are not assigned particular books to read or topics to write about. Instead, workshop teachers instruct students in making their own book and topic choices.

If your students will be reading from a textbook, whole-class novel, or other teacher-selected text, you might want to supplement that material with highly engaging, student-selected texts. If your students write primarily to assignments and prompts, you may want to give topic choice a try. (There are a few places within the book where strategies for managed topic choice is taught—so class topics can very much work.) Alternately, you might consider skipping ahead past the generating ideas lessons and into the planning and drafting ones.

Individual Levels of Reading and Writing

It's important to have students access work at their own level. When students are reading, encourage them to read books that they can read independently most of the time. If they do want to try to read books above their comfort zone, make sure to provide them with scaffolds. For example, if a student wants to read a fairly complex text on a topic of interest, it helps to explain that content knowledge can often lift our ability to read at higher levels than we typically can with an unfamiliar text. So we can help students build a text set for themselves, starting with very accessible texts, perhaps lower than their current reading ability, to help build foundational knowledge and vocabulary, then helping students to create stepping stones of other books on the topic, gradually building in complexity. As the student makes her way through each text, she gains content and vocabulary know-how that will help buoy her as she attempts to tackle the more complex syntax, text features, and concepts at higher levels. This work can also be supplemented with images, videos, and virtual trips to museums to add another layer of content knowledge with more modalities than the printed word.

Another way to help give students more access to nonfiction reading is to offer digital tools, such as e-books, apps that read aloud texts when needed, or help to easily find definitions or pronunciations of words. This works best when students are reading several titles on the same topic so that students can transfer their knowledge as they move from text to text, developing more and more independence as they go.

When considering individual support for writing, I always choose options that allow for the maximum level of independence and agency. So for example, instead of scribing for a student, I will work to teach the student how to use a keyboard, specialized word processing software such as Co:writer, or speech-to-text software so that the student can record his own writing. Rather than handing a student who needs support with organization a graphic organizer, I will show him options that he can make himself or else introduce a digital tool that he can use to choose his own graphic organizers. At every turn, I want to consider what obstacles might be getting in the way of my writers and what tools or scaffolds I can offer to help students move over those obstacles with maximum independence.

This also might be a nice time to try some small-group reading or writing work to support student learning goals as well. Since so many students will be invested in the work they are doing, teaching them specific strategies and skills that allow them to access the texts they most want to read will be highly engaging work.

If your students are reading textbooks or whole-class books, there's a fairly decent chance that some students might find the texts too challenging or too easy. However, since the reading strategies work on any text, you can likely teach them within textbooks or whole-class novels. You might also consider teaching them within a content area—such as science or social studies— whether you have trade books and choice or not. Additionally, you might find that teaching informational reading and writing can offer an opportunity for you to supplement your current reading and writing instruction with accessible texts, even as a short two-week detour from the textbook.

It is equally important to honor students' individual levels as you are teaching writing. Their development as writers is paramount. Even if there are grade standards in mind, it is important to recognize that some students develop more quickly or slowly than their peers. Instead of insisting that students hit a prespecified level of writing, teachers should work with students individually to design personal goals.

Additional Components

Most workshop classrooms also include additional components outside of the workshop time, which cover other important literacy areas. Elements such as read aloud, word study, and even cursive writing are touched upon and utilized within the workshop, but more time is allotted to them outside of the workshop. Some of the lessons in this book contain references to additional components, such as texts read aloud to students prior to the lesson.

If you currently are not teaching using the workshop model, you might wish to consider dabbling in some of those additional components. The chances are good that you probably already read aloud to your students, but perhaps you could more actively link that read-aloud work with your reading and writing lessons. You might already incorporate spelling, conventions, vocabulary, and the like into your day, but perhaps as you are working through some of the ideas in this book, you might consider more closely aligning the work between the study of words and the study of reading and writing those words.

Preparing for Writing . . . *First*

Okay, so what does it mean for us when we prepare for the writing work first, with an eye to how it will also feed the reading work? To begin with, you will want to decide what sort of writing you want your students to do. The lessons in this book will support the following:

- Nonfiction/informational books of personal expertise
- Content area (social studies, science, etc.) books
- Research reports
- Articles
- Oral reports

Of course, you can revise any lesson, material suggested, or book referenced to have it better suit your needs. The assumption in the lessons is that students are picking their own topics, even in cases where the students are writing within a class topic, such as electricity. In that case, the students might choose a subtopic, such as currents or light. This is because research (Bonyadi & Zeinalpur, 2014; Graves, 1983; Kohn, 1993) and personal experience show that students write best when they have an element of choice and agency in their projects. When students receive topic choice, whether writing in their dominant or even a new language (Bonzo, 2008), they are more likely to write with more volume, fluency, and intentionality. One of the easiest ways to improve student writing quality is to allow them to choose their topic (or in some cases, subtopic).

Next, after you have chosen the type of writing, you will want to choose mentor texts—that is, texts written by professional authors in the *style* and *form* you would like your students to write. Many educators in the writing workshop community have come to believe that the best mentor texts are on a topic *different from* the one the student is writing on. This is because it lessens the chances students will feel compelled to over-rely on (and perhaps unintentionally plagiarize) a mentor text.

Many of the texts you choose for the reading component could be good candidates for mentor texts. A few key features of strong mentor texts include the following:

- Demonstrates the *qualities* of writing that will be taught

- Is about the length that students will write

- Is slightly above students' current writing abilities

- Will be readable to many students

- Is a text that you and your students like and will find engaging through repeated readings

- Could be a text written by current or previous students

You will also want to gather any supplies necessary for students to use while writing and for you to use while teaching. For the students, you will want to be sure they have the following:

- Writing notebooks

- Plenty of loose paper

- Folders

- Pens (ideally, a variety of colors available)

- Sticky notes

- Highlighters

If you plan to have students work and publish digitally, you will want to organize those tools as well. (See the description of digital options discussed later in this chapter.) Additionally, some of the lessons use building blocks such as Snap Cubes, unit blocks, or LEGO bricks. They can be helpful manipulatives for writing instruction. If you plan to teach research as part of this unit, you might want to consider gathering paper, digital, and artifact-based research materials (such as objects, photographs, etc.) into baskets, bins, or other easy-to-navigate containers.

For yourself, you will want to gather chart paper or whatever tools you plan to use in order to visibly record your writing instruction. You will also want to think about—and perhaps prepare—a demonstration text you will use throughout the lessons. I have a demonstration text threaded through many of the lessons that you can certainly use, or you can revise it to more closely match what you and your students need. Some teachers like to closely model their demonstration text off their individual class's needs. I think this is a wonderful idea and can be easily done by gathering a few samples of a range of your students' initial informational writing tries.

Preparing for Reading

As you may have imagined, preparing for reading will require a bit more legwork. Perhaps the biggest bulk of preparation will go into gathering texts for students to read. In the appendix, you will find a list of recommended texts as a good starting place.

The reading work in this book can be done in a variety of ways with any number of text types or situations. You might wish to teach the lessons in a pure workshop model where students choose the texts they are reading. You might want to teach the lessons as a unit, as an overlay to a content-specific unit. You might also teach many of these lessons while students are using a textbook. A few possibilities for texts that can be used for the reading components in this book include the following:

- High-interest trade books at accessible reading levels for each student

- Trade books organized around a class content area (such as medieval Europe or human anatomy)

- Articles and permission-granted photocopied material

- Online resources

- Textbooks

- E-books or apps or websites connected to digital libraries

You will also want to gather read-aloud texts, independent reading texts, and additional reading tools. Since these components are so essential, let's look at each category in more detail.

Read-Aloud Texts

This book does not directly address read alouds. However, many of the lessons assume that books have previously been read aloud to students, and these books are mentioned directly. Ideally, most workshop teachers have additional time outside of the workshop time to read aloud selected texts to their students. This period can take anywhere from five to thirty minutes, and it usually includes discussion time.

It is not possible to overstate how important reading aloud to students on a daily basis is to their language, reading, and social-emotional development. Additionally, daily read alouds of texts that are the same genre the students are writing allow students to get a deep sense of how informational texts can be written, as well as to help them envision what is possible for their own writing.

Select possible read-aloud texts that will become touchstone texts that you and your class will refer to again and again throughout the unit. Some authors such as Melissa Stewart, Steve Bloom, and Penny Colman particularly lend themselves to being read aloud.

Some of the best read-aloud books are ones that lend themselves to being performed by a reader (you) and lead to a shared experience with an audience (the students). Specifically, they possess the following:

- Have language that sounds good orally

- Contain engaging content

- Allow teachers to demonstrate to students how to orchestrate skills by showing how in one page a reader might predict, synthesize, question, and determine importance in concert

Some efficient teachers can double-dip their reading and writing texts, opting to read aloud a text that will be used as a writing mentor but also allows for reading work. Throughout this book, whenever possible, I recommend texts that will work for both reading and writing instruction and are particularly fun or lyrical when read aloud.

Independent Reading Texts

It is also essential to gather texts for the students to read independently and with their partners or clubs. If you decide to have your students read their science or social studies textbook, it is still a good idea to make a variety of trade books, magazines, and online resources available to complement that content. Ideally, you will have enough texts to keep students reading independently the entire time, but if this is not possible, you might wish to organize your texts in such a way that students can swap with each other or else partner with another class and swap. Some teachers ask students to lend texts from home; others use a teacher library card to check out books from the local library. In any event, you will want to be sure students have enough to read through the course of the unit.

Additional Reading Tools

You will also want to gather other reading tools for you and your students. For your teaching, these might be many of the same tools you use in your writing instruction, including chart paper, sticky notes, highlighters, and chart markers. As well, your students will need the following:

- Reading notebooks
- Sticky notes
- Index cards
- Highlighters
- Reading logs
- Book sleeves or another way to keep the books they are currently reading together

You might also consider investing in baskets that can help store and organize books. What is most important is that students have ready access to a variety of reading materials that they can easily access independently.

Timing and Scheduling

In general, many workshop practitioners recommend forty-five minutes or more for writing workshop most days of the week and approximately sixty minutes or more for reading workshop most days of the week. Depending on your school schedule and situation, this may be way too much or not nearly enough. However, the lessons and activities in this book are designed around those guidelines, so if you have less or more time available, you will want to shrink or expand accordingly.

As noted, this book is designed for the writing lesson to be taught before the paired reading lesson. This can happen on the same day, but it is also possible to give the writing lesson a day or two ahead of the reading lesson. In some cases, I could even imagine the writing lessons being taught weeks or months before and simply referred back to explicitly when the paired reading lesson comes up. If you are teaching a particular subject or discipline, you might teach several other content-specific lessons in between the writing and reading paired lessons.

Note: Even though daily read-aloud time is not specifically mentioned in these lessons, it is absolutely essential to your students' development as readers and writers and for their overall academic success. Even though this book does not specifically call out read aloud, please know that there is very little that we can do that has greater impact on our students' literacy.

Digital Considerations

In each section of this book, you will find lessons that are specifically aimed at classrooms where digital tools will be utilized. While the rest of the book is not written specifically for schools that are using digital tools, there is no reason why all of the non-digital-specific lessons could not be entirely taught using digital tools. In fact, if your school is a one-to-one school, you will likely find many of the lessons intuitively easy to teach digitally, or at least you will find it simple to offer digital options to your students. There are many different ways this can look, and if you are already digitally savvy, it is likely that you already translate work to digital options pretty regularly.

For those of you who would like some ideas to start with, here are a few options you might consider.

1. Choose the form of the writing notebook. Many teachers like the portability and inexpensive nature of the paper notebook, which allows students to take it anywhere from the soccer field to the swimming pool. Other teachers swear by the generative powers of the old-fashioned pen in hand. However, you might decide to go with a digital platform if your students have access to portable digital devices that are able to travel back and forth from home to school. There are many notebook applications that students can use for generative work, such as Evernote and Noteshelf. Some teachers prefer students stay in the same word-processing application

throughout the writing process—including what is commonly called the "notebook phase." This is definitely an option; however, many teachers find that moving from one format to the next is helpful to symbolically differentiate between the generative and drafting process. You could, of course, also give students the choice of what tool works best for them.

2. Choose a word-processing program that allows students to track changes or to save multiple versions of drafts so that revision and editing moves can be easily tracked. Some teachers like Google Docs because of its history features. Others prefer to use Word and insist that students use the track changes feature.

3. Have students read online as well as e-books. There are a multitude of texts and endless libraries available. Most popular nonfiction books have a digital component that can be found on your local public library's site (or use a site like Overdrive to allow even easier access to public library sources). Popular websites that include great digital reading for students, such as *National Geographic for Kids* and *Time for Kids*, are worth bookmarking, as well as linking to specific article sites that are written for adults but sometimes have kid-accessible articles, such as *The Smithsonian*, CNN.com, and the *New York Times* Science section. One of the huge advantages of having access to digital tools is the ability to access multimodal texts involving hyperlinks, video, infographics, and the like. It is important to note that current research also suggests that reading comprehension is affected by the use of digital tools. Because of that, teachers should actively teach reading comprehension specific to reading e-books, as well as online texts that are multimodal. In other words, while digital reading is important, so is our active monitoring of and teaching into it.

4. Make paper books and texts available and accessible as well. Even if your school has decided to be all digital all of the time, it is important that there is some time for students to work with analogue materials as well. We want them to notice the differences between reading paper and digital texts—both the pros and the cons. Because the research is still ongoing around reading and writing digitally, we want to make sure our students are able to fluently move between both.

Providing Access to All Students

Lastly, you will notice as you make your way through these lessons that a majority of them should be accessible to most students. This is by design.

I have a particular passion, developed over years of being an educator and a parent, to make learning accessible to as many students as possible. Luckily, the workshop model is naturally accessible because students always have choice, and we end lessons by reminding students that they have a repertoire of strategies they can choose from. However, if you do not typically use the workshop model or if you are trying it for the first time, this can feel very different from assigning something and expecting that all students will be working on the same goal and activity for an entire class period. The good news is that many of the techniques described in this book that make the lessons accessible are also techniques that can be applied outside of the workshop model.

Since the lessons rely on students' own writing pieces and independent reading texts, the strategies should be applicable to most situations. For lessons with concepts that are particularly challenging, I have included additional scaffolds, such as the following, to offer more access.

- Heavy use of teacher demonstration

- Guided practice whenever appropriate

- Plenty of opportunities for talk, sketching, using manipulatives and other ways of practicing skills

- A strong emphasis on engagement

- Use of multilevel texts

If you or your school employs the Universal Design for Learning Framework, you will find that most of the lessons align well or can be easily aligned with that framework.

How the Book Is Set Up

Each section in this book is set up to support a different part of the writing process.

Part 1: Lessons for Generating Ideas—and Interpreting Author's Purpose. The lessons in this section help you guide students to choose and rehearse their best informational writing ideas alongside interpreting an informational book's purpose in their reading life.

Part 2: Lessons for Drafting—and Understanding Author's Craft. This section contains a variety of techniques for drafting in compelling ways, as well as early front-end revision work paired with one of the trickiest things for students to understand as readers: an author's craft moves.

Part 3: Lessons for Revising for Power, Craft, Analysis, and Critique. Here, the lessons get meatier as the writing work takes on more importance and students learn to transfer their own choices as writers to the task of judging the choices of the authors whose work they are reading.

Part 4: Lessons to Prepare for Publication and the Scholarly Study of Texts. As you might imagine, these lessons are geared toward teaching students strategies for reflection as both writers and readers. Students see how their final decisions as writers have a direct effect on how their audience takes in their work. They also see how texts can be studied deeply long after they are finished and then use this study to make plans for future reading work.

My Hopes for This Book

First, it is my fondest hope that you and your students will walk away with the deep understanding that strong and aware writers become stronger and more aware readers. It is easy to go through life simply consuming at a surface level, whether it's a quick Internet read or a text from a friend, but when students become aware that producing and consuming are interconnected, they cannot help but look differently—whether critically or appreciatively—at every bit of writing they make or read.

Second, I hope that on both the reading and writing sides of the equation, your students learn to pay more attention to author's intent, craft, and meaning in informational texts. Often, fiction and poetry get all of the love, but there is much to learn about and deepen with information writing, which not only helps us get smarter but also has a unique way of allowing us to view the world through more wondrous, fact-focused eyes.

Third, I hope your students will find themselves regularly transferring the skills they learn from these informational lessons to other subject areas, genres, and situations. Once writers see how much better their reading can be if they make that jump, I want them to make similar connections across their subject areas, disciplines, hobbies, activities, and relationships with the view of what it looks like to be on *both* sides.

For most of my life, I considered myself a fiction writer. When I sat in front of my typewriter (and, later, my computer), I was drawn to creating characters, settings, and plots that were purely of my imagination. I loved to invent stories that set up readers to get lost in the pages. And while I have always been a lover of facts, the kind of person who enjoys spouting statistics and trivia at cocktail parties, the last kind of text I picked up to read in my spare time was anything informational (at least, so I thought). This carried through to my work in the classroom. I taught students to write and read in most of the major genres. However, the area where my passion was most on display was fiction.

Fast forward to my second career as a teacher who works with other teachers. Suddenly, as I was looking alongside teachers at ways to best teach nonfiction writing, I made the stunning discovery that I was in fact an informational writer and reader all along! When we began to think about what we did in our real lives as readers and writers, I saw that almost every day I wrote and read some sort of nonfiction text. Whether I was engaged with lessons, e-mails, articles, books about education, or *US Weekly*, I was regularly immersed in the world of information.

You, too, are no doubt more immersed in informational writing than you probably first assumed. Much of what is discussed in this chapter is gleaned from my own reading and writing life, as well as the reading and writing life of the countless amazing teachers I have been able to study alongside over the past several years. I hope that you will recognize yourself and your students in many of these lessons and that the material will resonate deeply with your goals for your own classroom.

PART 1

LESSONS FOR GENERATING IDEAS—AND INTERPRETING AUTHOR'S PURPOSE

What You Will Find in This Section

Writing. When writers of nonfiction texts first dig into writing, just as I did when I first began writing this book, they spend some time nailing down what exactly they want to write about. Whether this involves finding an angle inside of an assigned topic (e.g., a newspaper article or a science report) or reaching into the infinite list of possible topics to pluck one that feels right, getting a project started can be the most intimidating aspect of writing. In this section, I offer several strategies to make this generative aspect of the writing process more accessible.

Reading. The lessons in this section bridge the work the students are doing as writers to the work they can do as readers of nonfiction texts. The lessons demonstrate how what students have learned about generating topics can give them unique insights into the texts they are reading and help them develop strategies to comprehend texts more deeply.

When to Use These Lessons

As is the case with every section in this book, many of the lessons are applicable for almost all teaching situations. However, some are more tailored to more choice-driven units and others are better served if you teach them within a more narrowly defined topic-based unit (as in a social studies or science-based topic).

Preparing to Use the Lessons

There are a few things I recommend you do to prepare to teach the lessons in this chapter:

1. **Start thinking of possible topics you are an expert in, whether inside or outside of a content area.** Some people respond to this suggestion with, "But I'm not an expert at anything." This is, of course, not true. If you do find yourself stuck, try thinking about something you do on a daily basis. A good writing topic is something

that interests both you and your students. I often write about vermin and pests, but you could just as easily write about cooking or tennis or car mechanics or couponing. The topic matters less than the fact that you are interested in it.

2. **Let your students and your own interests guide you.** Freshen your classroom library with books, articles, and digital texts in a variety of topics on a variety of reading levels. Students naturally love to read nonfiction—if the nonfiction is compelling and well written. Many classrooms suffer from a dearth of nonfiction reading choices. Be sure to prepare for the reading lessons by bringing engaging nonfiction texts into the class.

3. **Organize the texts.** Arrange the shelves, baskets, or files so that books on the same or related topics are grouped together. This will make a lot of the work described in this chapter a little bit simpler. It is also worth considering ways to make your classroom text collection more enticing, whether creating student-curated sections or changing up the signs for baskets of books to have more intriguing titles or some other way that will make these nonfiction texts irresistible. You might also consider arranging a chunk of your collection according to reading levels in order to make them more accessible to students who need support in finding books that won't frustrate them with difficulty. Many schools prefer Fountas and Pinnell guided reading levels (*Guiding Readers and Writers* by Irene Fountas and Gay Su Pinnell, 2001), but, of course, there are several systems for leveling books to make sure students have scaffolding they might need for book choice. That said, levels are not the only way to make sure books are accessible to students. If your students will be reading digital texts, you will likely want to organize them into digital bins, on a class website or drive, or else consider other ways for students to find and access these texts.

4. **Organize your materials and reading time.** For more details on organizing your materials and reading time, please refer to the introduction.

As you move into these lessons, whether you are teaching them all or picking and choosing which ones to teach, keep an eye out for places that the reading and writing connections seem to be the smoothest and give your students and you the most energy. Ideally, the energy created at the beginning of any project can be expanded upon as the project progresses.

writing

AN AUTHOR'S EXPERTISE MATTERS

Lesson steps

1. Inform students they are launching a new unit on [insert unit topic here].

2. Explain that they will be writing about topics they know a lot about.

3. Prompt students to take a "thought journey" of their everyday lives, guiding them to picture certain situations and asking them specific questions to help them uncover their areas of expertise.

4. Using this guided practice, teach students to reflect on the areas in their lives where people come to them for more information.

5. Give students time to list or freewrite about topics they are known for during the rest of the class period.

What I Say to Students

As many of you know, we are beginning new writing pieces. But these pieces aren't just any kind of writing. These are pieces that are meant to teach and share knowledge with the world: your knowledge—those things you personally know so much about. Some people call these *nonfiction writing*. Others call them *informational*. But whatever you call them, they involve writing that is meant to teach.

I can see from some of your faces that you are thinking that I couldn't possibly be talking about you; after all, you're kids. How can you possibly be experts? But, it's true. Every one of us is an expert on something. Sometimes, we can be experts on something big and academic sounding—like maybe something we've studied in school or in a class, like photosynthesis or algebra. Or maybe it's something you love to do in your spare time, a sport you play, an art you make, or a responsibility you take on.

PURPOSE

Students learn that nonfiction writers often launch their writing projects off of their own knowledge base. They begin to think of and appreciate their areas of expertise, which could be the foundation for pieces of writing.

LESSON INTENDED FOR

- Personal expertise books
- Content-specific books or reports
- Oral reports
- Research reports
- Students at a wide range of levels

MATERIALS NEEDED

- A piece of chart paper, a document camera, or another place visible to all where you can write the guided practice questions you will use
- Students' writing notebooks (optional)

I'm going to ask you to go on a little "thought journey" with me. I'm going to ask you to take a tour of your life. You might want to close your eyes or stare at the ceiling or even jot things in your notebook as I do this. I will call out some ideas and questions to think about as you explore the areas in your life where you carry a lot of knowledge.

I'd like you to picture your home or someplace else you spend a lot of time—whole days. Can you picture it? For me it would be my apartment, where I spend most of my time when I'm not in school. Once you have it in your mind, look around. What do you see? One question you might ask yourself is this:

What activities do I do well here?

I know one thing I do really well is bake. Actually, I'm not just a good baker, but I'm also a really good candymaker. And I know that my friends and family often ask me for my recipes or to sample my treats. I see a few of you smiling—that's fantastic! I should add that if you get a good idea for writing, go ahead and jot it in your notebook if you'd like.

Now, let's continue our tour. I'd look you to look up and down and all around—on shelves and walls and under chairs, desks, and beds. What do you see? One question you might ask yourself is this:

What objects do I use all the time that I use well?

I know one thing I see in my mind's eye is my Metrocard because I take a bus or subway almost every day. This reminds me that people often ask me for subway tips or directions. I think I could definitely say that I'm a little famous with the people I know for how much I travel and how well I get around the subway.

Let's try another idea. You could answer this question in your mind's eye or else by looking in real life. I want you to look at yourself—the clothes you are wearing, your hands, your knees, and your hair. Ask yourself this question:

What do I notice about myself that says something about what I'm known for?

It could be that you have a scar on your knee that reminds you of your favorite skateboard trick. It could be the sparkles on your fingernails that remind you of how much you are into fashion. It could even be the shoes that you're wearing—either the style or the scuffs or even the kind of dirt they have accumulated in the grooves.

Now, let's try one more question—just in case it's helpful. Picture a conversation you had recently with friends or family. If you can, especially picture a conversation where people were coming to you for advice, or they were asking you questions. This could be grown-ups in your life or cousins or even little brothers and sisters. Then, ask yourself this:

What topic do the people in my life most ask me about? What do they see me as an expert in?

A few of you might have noticed that you are getting a lot of ideas—more than you could possibly keep going in your head. You might want to use this opportunity to list your possible informational book ideas in your notebook. On the other hand, some of you might feel very different. You don't have a ton of ideas. You have one or two that are burning you up. You know what you want to write about now. If that's the case, you can take this class time to write long about the topic that is at the forefront of your mind right now as a sort of rehearsal to see if this topic really is the one you want to work on.

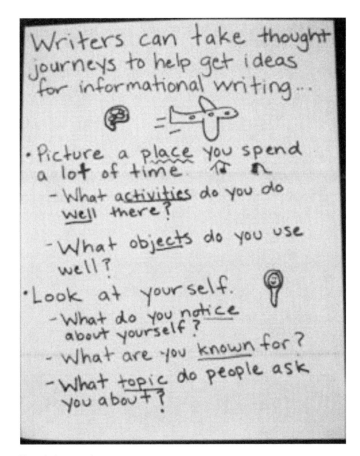

Thought journey chart

Reading
CONSIDERING THE SOURCE

PURPOSE

Students learn how to evaluate authorship of nonfiction texts.

This lesson will be one of a few you will want to teach about the importance of considering the source of the information when reading any text.

LESSON INTENDED FOR

- Reading high-interest nonfiction
- Trade books
- Articles
- Online sources
- Students who are reading texts where there is information on the author available

MATERIALS NEEDED

- Your demonstration reading text, with a clearly written author biography that shows that the author has some expertise on the topic (for this lesson, I use *How to Make a Universe With 92 Ingredients* by Adrian Dingle)
- Students' independent reading texts

Lesson steps

1. Use an imagined scenario where students have to decide whose advice to seek based on a particular context or situation.

2. Explain that readers should find out about an author's areas of expertise.

3. Tell students that knowing the author's background can help let the reader in on the author's possible perspective.

4. Have students spend the rest of the time independently reading, referring to the author's background when appropriate.

What I Say to Students

I have another little thought experiment to try with you today. Let's say you wanted to buy a new video game with money you received for your birthday, but you weren't sure which one to buy. You wanted to learn more information on the options. Who should you ask if these were your choices?

A) Your best friend, who loves to play video games

B) A person who works at the video game store

C) Our school principal

D) A video game designer

Now, before you answer the question, I want you to think a little bit about what you want to learn, which is what video game should you buy. Each resource has different information. Some of it is better than others for the purposes that you might have.

For example, let's say that your best friend loves to play video games and is about the same age, so this resource can give you a player's point of view.

Your principal can maybe tell you what games she's heard kids talking about (or has taken away from them), but as far as I know, she is not a huge player herself. The video game designer knows how games work, what goes into designing them, and anything about the games she's designed. But she might not know as much about games she hasn't directly worked on. In contrast, the person who works at the video game store knows about all of the latest games, which ones are most popular, and what the prices are.

Talk to your partner about why you might choose each resource and why. And—if you would want to talk to more than one resource, share why you think that.

[Circulate and listen in as students discuss. Then call them back together.]

So here's the thing: it kind of doesn't really matter which resource or resources you said you would consult with because everyone has a different agenda, as well as different preferences. However, it's important to know that's exactly the way readers can consider the nonfiction books they are reading. We consider our own preferences and our own agendas. Then we look at those alongside the backgrounds, experiences, and agendas of the authors of the texts we are considering reading. When we find a good match, we know this is a good text for us. For example—let me show you this book.

[Hold up demonstration text.]

This book is all about the elements. It's called *How to Make a Universe With 92 Ingredients* by Adrian Dingle. If I just want to learn about the topic—all aspects of it—I'm in a pretty good spot. But let me just check the back cover and see who wrote this book—if the author is an expert on this topic or an expert on informational writing . . .

[Open up back flap of book and look at back cover. Read aloud the author's description.]

> Adrian Dingle is a high school chemistry teacher. He was born in England but has extensive experience teaching science in both the United States and the United Kingdom. He is the award winning author of several chemistry books at the junior level, including *The Periodic Table: Elements With Style*, and also has a number of textbooks to his credit.

Knowing about the author, what his or her experience is with the topic and with writing in general, isn't going to make me read a book or not read a book, but it will help me to get a sense of where the author is coming from. It gives me some background that I can hold in my mind as a reader. It might tell me if this author has a particular affinity for a topic or a particular dislike. This can affect the way the author writes about the topic, and as a reader it's important for me to keep that information in my mind as I read.

When I read about Adrian Dingle just now, I realized that he has quite a bit of science expertise. Also important, he is a teacher, so he brings expertise of how to speak with and teach children. That makes me trust his information is going to be accurate and also sets me up to expect that I will learn a lot from his book.

This is different from if I just jumped online and read the first article that popped up on an Internet search. Sometimes, especially if the information is crowdsourced, like a lot of people shared their information and pieced it together, like they do for Wikipedia, it is challenging to know who the author is and what his or her area of expertise might be. In that case, while I might learn a lot from that source, I might not give it as much credit as another verifiable and definitely identified as expert source.

When you go off to read today, take a few seconds to check out the background of the author of the book you're reading. You might want to even compare two texts with authors with different backgrounds. What do you notice about the depth of information? Or how the different authors treat the material?

And in general, as you read today and in the future, you'll want to be aware of the background and experience of the people whose pieces you are reading, whenever possible.

Partners planning their resources

writing

WRITE ABOUT WHAT YOU TAKE FOR GRANTED

Lesson steps

1. Tell students about the famous advice almost every writer hears: "Write what you know."

2. Set them up to work with partners to brainstorm ideas for areas of expertise.

3. Encourage students to record their ideas in their notebooks.

PURPOSE

Students learn the advantages of "writing what you know."

LESSON INTENDED FOR

- Personal expertise books
- Oral reports
- Students at a wide range of levels

MATERIALS NEEDED

- Students' writing notebooks

What I Say to Students

One of the famous pieces of advice writers hear is to write what you know. And it's absolutely a wise piece of advice most of the time. Yet when it comes to nonfiction, sometimes writers have a blind spot about topics they know the deepest; for me, it's as though the topic is so enmeshed in my everyday life, maybe it seems too ordinary to write about.

So today we are going to lean on our partners to help remind us of areas of expertise in our lives—people, places, and things in our lives that we know a lot about. Maybe these are even areas we are famous for knowing a lot about. Earlier today, when I first got to school, I asked Ms. Roberts what she thought I was an expert on, and she mentioned coffee, books, ferrets, my bathroom, and baking. She then went on to say more about why she thought I was an expert on those things. I was a little surprised, but when I really thought about it, I realized that she was right—I did know a lot about each of those things. Enough to write whole books about them!

Today, I would like you to go off with your partners or groups and take turns talking about what you know about each other's areas of expertise. When people say you are an expert at something, ask them to talk about why they think that.

[As students speak with their partners, circulate and listen in, prompting the conversations if needed.]

When you're done talking, take a few minutes to return to your writing notebook, and jot some of the things you do know about each of those topics. Explore a bit, and see if one of those topics seems like it feels right.

A student brainstorming in her notebook

Reading

LEARNING UNEXPECTED THINGS FROM FAMILIAR TOPICS

Lesson steps

1. Give an example of when you were surprised by someone you thought you knew.

2. Explain how we can be surprised by information we find in books, even about topics we think we know really well.

3. Demonstrate how this might look with a text excerpt, modeling how we might first think of the information we know, and then pause and take note when we are surprised.

4. Send students to try this in the information books they are reading.

PURPOSE

Students learn that even when they are reading about a familiar topic, they need to prepare to assimilate new information.

LESSON INTENDED FOR

- Reading high-interest nonfiction
- Trade books
- Articles
- Content area trade books
- Textbooks

MATERIALS NEEDED

- Your class read aloud, with a page marked that you haven't yet read, to use during the demonstration (in this lesson, I use an excerpt from the book *The Story of Salt* by Mark Kurlansky)
- Informational texts the students are currently reading (one per child)

What I Say to Students

Have you ever come home and found someone you know really well—a parent, a brother or sister, or a babysitter—doing or saying something really unexpected? For instance, I remember one time I came home from school and I found my parents swing dancing in the kitchen. They were twirling around, and my father even dipped my mother! I was shocked. I had known my parents my whole life, but I didn't even know they knew how to dance. But in that moment, I learned something completely new about them, something that changed the way I held onto the information I thought I knew about them.

The same is true when you are reading a book or an article about a topic you think you know everything about. It's like you're going along *[hold up book and act out reading]* and you're thinking, "Yep—knew that. Yep, knew that too." But then suddenly, even though you think you knew everything, you come across a section where you might be surprised. Let me show you what I mean.

[Hold up text.]

I thought I knew a lot about salt. But when I started reading this book, *The Story of Salt* (**Mark Kurlansky, G.P. Putnam's & Sons © 2006**), I was really surprised. Let me read you an excerpt:

> Salt is the only rock eaten by human beings. In fact, all mammals, including humans, need to eat sodium chloride in order to live. Sodium chloride is needed for breathing and for digestion, and without salt the body could not transport nourishment, oxygen, or nerve impulses, which means that the body would not function at all.

Now, I'll be honest—I thought I knew everything I needed to know about salt. But luckily, I kept my mind open, so I wasn't sleepwalking while I was reading. I was awake and ready to be surprised—ready to learn. So suddenly I learned that we all need salt in order to live—the same way we need food, water, and breathing!

What's interesting about this is that I need to have my mind ready to learn more things. I can't just gloss over my reading, because if I do, I might miss some new information, which would not only make me even more knowledgeable about this topic but also make me a stronger reader. And I believe that learning more information on a topic we already know so much about happens more often than we'd care to admit. So I'd like us to all try it right now. I'd like you to grab one of the nonfiction books you are reading right now, and I'd like you to have your mind open and ready as you read— open for some new information that you might find unexpected. Then, I want you to make a note of that new information and see where you place it in your mind. How does it affect your thinking and reading going forward?

Student reading with his mind open

THE RELATIONSHIP BETWEEN AN AUTHOR'S PASSIONS AND STANCE

Lesson steps

1. Tell a story that makes the point that the best writing comes from the heart.

2. Demonstrate using your own writing. Model writing about topics you have a deep affinity for.

3. Remind students that they have a few strategies you already taught them for finding a good topic and that another strategy they might choose to use is to write about things they care deeply about.

PURPOSE

Students consider their passions as possible topics to explore for nonfiction writing.

LESSON INTENDED FOR

- Personal expertise books
- Oral reports
- Students at a wide range of levels

MATERIALS NEEDED

- Your demonstration writing notebook
- Students' writing notebooks

What I Say to Students

There is a woman named Georgia Heard who is a poet and also a teacher of writing. She shows students that one way they can get poetry writing going is to make a map of their hearts. Some of you might have even made maps of your hearts at some point in writing workshop. You start by making a quick sketch of a heart outline. Then, you divide the heart into different sections to help you think about what people, places, and things you love. Those loves, or what some people might call *affinities*, are great places to look for ideas for possible poems. In the same way, your heart is a great place to look for ideas for informational texts.

Think about it. When you are excited and passionate about something and you are sharing that something with someone else, you are almost bouncing out of your seat. And when you are so excited about something, your enthusiasm is contagious. The people listening to you can't help but get excited. The same is true when we are writing. When we write about the topics we feel deep passion or affinity for, we are setting ourselves and our readers up for a great time.

Let me show you what I mean with my own writing.

[Turn to the demonstration notebook, and jot while thinking out loud.]

I have a few things that really make me happy—some real passions in my life. Like books—I cannot possibly love books more. I love the smell of them. I love the feel of them. I love even how they are made. I love paper ones and e-books . . . Okay—so let me stop and jot a bit of that down before I get into another passion of mine—which is ferrets.

I think ferrets are the perfect pet. I've loved them for years. They are so fun to play with. They're easy to take care of . . . I could go on and on.

I think you all see what's happening here—how I'm jotting some of my affinities and a few notes about them. And as I do that, it's giving me even more ideas to write about.

Some of you already know what you want to write about and just want me to stop talking so you can get down to it. And in that case, don't let me keep you. But, if you're not 100 percent, remember all of the strategies I've taught you in this class and ones you might remember from when you were learning about writing in other grades. Any of those strategies can work for today. Or you might decide to try what I showed you today and think about some of your affinities and jot some things down about them.

No matter what you write today, what way you decide to get yourself going, I am so excited to read what you've written!

Passions chart

Reading

IDENTIFYING AN AUTHOR'S STANCE

Lesson steps

1. Define the term *affinity* for students, and explain how it is related to our stances and biases. Explain that all authors, including ourselves, have these stances.

2. Together, look for other authors' clues to their own biases.

3. Demonstrate by reading an excerpt with an eye toward the author's stance.

4. Guide students to work with a partner on a whole-class shared text, preferably one that is familiar, to read through the lens of authorial stance.

5. Send students off to read their informational texts in the future with a continued awareness that all authors have stances.

PURPOSE

Students learn to look for an author's stance on a topic.

LESSON INTENDED FOR

- Reading high-interest nonfiction
- Trade books
- Articles
- Content area trade books
- Textbooks

MATERIALS NEEDED

- A small sampling of text excerpts your students have read or have heard read aloud (for this lesson, I chose *The Story of Salt* by Mark Kurlansky and *Oh, Rats!* by Albert Marrin)

What I Say to Students

Earlier we looked at how our own affinities—the things that we as authors have a strong liking for—can help us to develop ideas to write about. As many of you have probably guessed, the feelings an author has about a subject can definitely affect his or her writing. Some people call that an *angle*. Other people call it a *stance*. Either term indicates that even though we like to think that nonfiction writers are strictly limited to facts only—that they don't have any bias whatsoever—the truth is that we all have a bias, which affects the way we present information to the world. All authors do.

So today we're going to talk about how knowing that all writers have affinities (and dislikes) can help us as readers keep on the lookout for the author's stance. And knowing this can also help us read cautiously, knowing that what we like or dislike is naturally going to have some effect on the work that we create too.

One way we can spot authors' stances is to keep our own author hats on. Remember what you wrote about your own topic (whether you loved it or hated it) and consider the choices you made as an author; these are the same choices all authors could make.

I thought we could try a bit of this together. Let's read another excerpt from *The Story of Salt* and think to ourselves, "What is this author's stance or angle?"

> The ancient Egyptians save salted food for both the living and the dead. Egyptian tombs have been found that are filled with urns of preserved foods that were meant to help the dead on their journey to the underworld.
>
> Dead bodies were also cleaned and salted to be preserved for eternity. Without salt, there would have been no mummies.

[Give students a few minutes to talk out what they think.]

Let's record a few of the possibilities you came up with:

> Mark Kurlansky's Angle:
>
> * Salt is useful.
>
> * Salt has been used by humans for a long time because it's so useful.
>
> * Salt was used by Egyptians for mummies and to prepare mummies for the afterlife—showing examples of just how useful even ancient people thought it was.

Now, let's reread an excerpt from another text we've read a lot, *Oh, Rats!* (Albert Marrin, Dutton Children's Books © 2006). Let's look to see what you think this author's angle might be, now that you know about how authors carry their affinities into their writing and how it might affect their angles.

[Share the excerpt.]

> To permit civilians to go about in safety, land mines must be removed. Experts detect mines with metal detectors or by crawling

on their hands and knees, carefully probing with knives. When they find one, they dig it up and disable its fuse. Sometimes a wrong move sets a mine off, killing them instantly.

The African giant pouch rat can detect mines more easily and safely than any humans. . . . Attached to a leash held by a handler, it lopes across a field and keeping its sensitive snout to the ground, sniffs for TNT, the explosive used in mines. Weighing just three pounds, the rat is too light to set off mines accidentally.

Please take a few minutes to discuss the angle with a partner.

[Give students a few minutes to talk out what they think. Listen in.]

Let's record a few of your theories about the author's angle.

- Mines are dangerous.

- Rats can help keep people safe.

- Rats can do things humans can't.

The next time you are reading an informational text, you'll want to add being aware of the author's stance or angle to your list of things you can do to strengthen your reading self.

Reading across a stack of text in the company of a friend

Writing

NARROWING DOWN A BROAD TOPIC

PURPOSE

Students learn how to look at the big topic they are studying and narrow it down to a smaller, more manageable subtopic.

LESSON INTENDED FOR

- Oral reports
- Topic-assigned writing
- Content-specific writing
- Students at a wide range of levels

MATERIALS NEEDED

- Your demonstration writing notebook
- Your sample content area notes (created ahead of time)
- Texts and resources on the class topic that can be used to model
- "How Informational Writers Can Narrow Their Topics" chart (on this page through the next)

Available for download at **resources.corwin.com/ writersreadbetter**

Lesson steps

1. Explain that one way information writers can strengthen their writing is by moving from broad topics to narrow ones.

2. Introduce steps, preferably using a chart or other visual, that students can follow in order to narrow down their topics.

3. Model quickly, using the introduced steps to narrow down demonstration topic.

4. Encourage students to consider trying this with their own projects.

 ## What I Say to Students

We've been studying weather for some time, this year and many years before this. It's probably one of the topics you've studied every year in school. We've done experiments, gone on field trips, read lots and lots of books, and I feel like each of us could write a very nice book on the overall topic of weather. However, I also think that you are able to do so much more than write a very nice book. You can each write your own amazing books based on your own personal areas of interest, especially if you choose to write with great detail about a smaller aspect of your topic.

Let's look at one great strategy that can help you narrow a large topic into a smaller, more focused topic.

[Display this chart, which you can download from the companion website:]

How Informational Writers Can Narrow Their Topics

- Step 1: Gather notes and important reading that you've done on the topic.

- Step 2: Review materials and mark up places that feel exciting or interesting.

- Step 3: Look across the mark-ups. Is there a pattern? Does one subtopic seem to be more intriguing than the next? Choose that subtopic.

- Step 4: Try a fast draft to see if this subtopic can become the main topic.

Writers, I'm going to try to do just that. I have all of my materials right here. Because some of them are paper and some of them are digital, I'm going to have to mark them up differently. On my paper texts, I'm going to need to use a sticky note. On my digital texts, I'm going to need to highlight.

[Model a page or two of quick rereading and marking.]

Next, I'm looking for any pattern or to see if something catches my eye. For example, I noticed that I have a few places where I marked something about tornadoes, but I also seem to have a lot of places marked whenever my notes of texts mention hurricanes. That makes me think that hurricanes would be a possible topic for me to narrow down to. So I'm going to make a note of that possibility.

Now I'm ready to do a quick draft just to see if I have enough to say on this topic to work with it. Let's see.

[Pick up a pen, and begin to draft. Then, stop after just a few sentences, which should be enough to give students a sense of what you're writing but not so much that it will take a lot of time to do it.]

I think you all can imagine how my new narrowed-down writing might go. And I can tell that many of you are thinking you might want to try this too. After all, the more you narrow the topic, the easier it will be to write it well.

Reading

UNDERSTANDING TOPICS
AND SUBTOPICS

PURPOSE

Students make a direct connection between the ordinate and subordinate development work they are doing in writing and the topics and subtopics they will encounter in the texts they read.

LESSON INTENDED FOR

- Reading high-interest nonfiction
- Trade books
- Articles
- Content area trade books
- Textbooks
- Students who are reading at a guided reading level M and above or are able to tackle books with more words and pages, less picture support

MATERIALS NEEDED

- A sample of text your students have read or have heard read aloud that contains headings and/ or subheadings (not all informational texts contain these, so you might want set these aside ahead of the lesson; for this lesson, I use *Thunderstorms* by Chana Stiefel)

Lesson steps

1. Make a connection to narrowing down a topic to subtopics in writing.

2. Explain that when reading, we can notice other writers' choices for narrowing down a topic.

3. Study a familiar book's table of contents or other breakdown of subtopics.

4. Ask students to try noticing the subtopics in the books and other texts they read.

What I Say to Students

Earlier we talked about how writers decide which small slice of a big topic they want to write about. Now, let's keep thinking about this decision making as we go into reading someone's text: You are actually reading another author's decision of whether or not to focus on a big topic or subtopic. For example, a book on rainforest animals might have started out in the author's mind as a book on all aspects of the rainforest, including plants, weather, and preservation efforts.

Textbooks are good examples of a big topic and then smaller subtopics. For example, we're reading a textbook called *Science*, and each chapter is all about something different about science. Each chapter is a subtopic. But, it doesn't just happen in textbooks. Today, I want to remind you that every informational piece you read has a writer behind it who had to make decisions about the topics and subtopics that would be included (or not included) in the text.

Let's take a look together at *Thunderstorms* by Chana Stiefel (Chana Stiefel, Scholastic © 2009). If we look at the table of contents for this book, we can see some of the topics and subtopics that she has included, as well as what she has not included. I want you to look over this table of contents, and see what decisions you think the author made about what topics to address.

[Share contents page.]

1. Storm Brewing—How does a thunderstorm form?

2. Zap! Flash! Boom!—What is a severe thunderstorm?

3. Surviving Storms—Can people survive lightning, hail, and tornadoes?

4. Weather Watchers—How do scientists predict wild weather?

5. Run for Cover—What's the best place to be during a thunderstorm?

Please discuss this briefly with a partner.

[Listen in, and then, call them back together.]

Many of you noticed that there's an emphasis on humans and storms. Now, please work with your partner to study the headings and subheadings of other texts, considering why the authors of those books might have made those decisions.

Studying a table of contents and other front matter takes time.

Writing

THE ROLE OF STRUCTURE IN INFORMATIONAL TEXTS

PURPOSE

Students learn to use structural exploration as a strategy.

LESSON INTENDED FOR

- Personal expertise books
- Oral reports
- Topic-assigned writing
- Content-specific writing
- Students at all levels

MATERIALS NEEDED

- A class topic and some subtopics that can be used for whole-class practice.
- Topics and subtopics recorded on index cards, sentence strips, or digital cards (ideally, they can be manipulated in a physical way)
- Images of food ingredients from a popular fast-food restaurant (optional)

Lesson steps

1. Tell a story about a time where the same ingredients were made into different dishes.

2. Explain how structure has the same effect on the writing we can do.

3. Guide the students through trying this out by practicing on a class topic.

4. Note how simply changing the structure can completely change the type of piece a writer writes.

5. Encourage students to explore structure in their own pieces.

What I Say to Students

Just this weekend I was visiting my brother and his family, and we were so hungry that we stopped at Taco Bell. Everyone in my family ordered something different. One of my sons ordered a taco. The other one ordered a burrito. I ordered the fanciest nachos they had. When we looked at all of our food, we realized that almost all of them had the same few ingredients.

[Project images or a list of ingredients.]

Here's what we had.

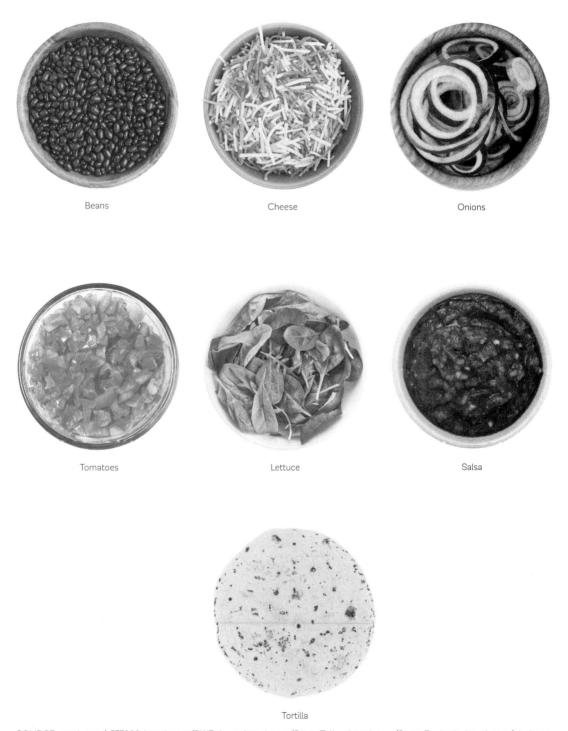

Beans

Cheese

Onions

Tomatoes

Lettuce

Salsa

Tortilla

SOURCE: stock.com/v777999, istock.com/BWFolsom, istock.com/Diana Taliun, istock.com/PhotoEuphoria, istock.com/vitalssss, istock.com/BWFolsom, and istock.com/duckycards.

The only thing that made a dish different was the way those ingredients were prepared and the order they were placed into the dish. And that, of course, got me thinking about how we organize things as information writers. At the beginning of a writing project, when we have a ton of information—or ingredients—there are so many different ways the writing can end up, just based on the treatment and placement of those ingredients.

The same is true when we are writing informational texts. We have a whole refrigerator full of facts, but the thing we make with it is completely affected by the way we put it together—the structure. Today, I want us to try doing some of that structuring together. I want us to take a topic we all know so well we could write a book together about it because we are all experts in it. The topic is our school's cafeteria.

[Have the class brainstorm a list of subtopics. Write them in a location where everyone can see them.]

Breakfast

Lunch

Drinks

Servers

Students

Lines

Tables

Recycling

Trash Cans

Compost

Food

Students

Salad Bar

Hot Food

Desserts

Trays

So, we could—but we don't have to—use each of these subtopics in our draft of our table of contents. You might even be looking at this list right now thinking that there are things missing. And you can feel free to add some things. But you might also be looking at this and thinking of possible ways to order these subtopics and the information that might be under them. Can you right now, with someone sitting near you, imagine one way a class book on our school cafeteria could go?

[After students finish talking, share a few of their overheard plans.]

One option I heard was to change the book to be not just the cafeteria—but cafeteria food. So it would go like this:

1. Breakfast
2. Lunch
3. Drinks
4. Hot Food
5. Salad Bar
6. Desserts

Another option I heard was to combine some of the subtopics together under other subtopics. So another partnership said this:

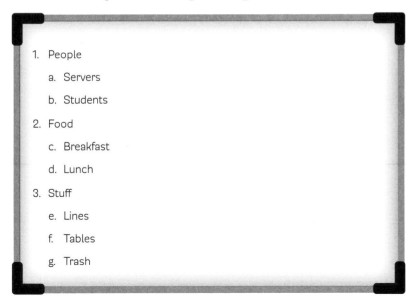

1. People
   a. Servers
   b. Students
2. Food
   c. Breakfast
   d. Lunch
3. Stuff
   e. Lines
   f. Tables
   g. Trash

What I want you to notice is that those two options, with the same ingredients to choose from, would make very different books. When you are thinking of possible structures for your own books, you might want to consider that. I encourage you today to try your topic out in a few different configurations of subtopics

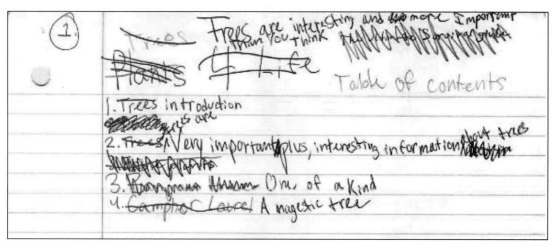

Brianna experiments with her table of contents for her book on trees.

Reading

CONSIDERING HOW CHOICES IN STRUCTURE AFFECT MEANING

Lesson steps

1. Make a direct connection between the work students did with structure in their writing and the structure decisions authors have made.

2. Guide students to study one familiar text and the way it is structured.

3. Share another text on the same topic as the first text that has a different structure. Guide students to notice the effects those different structures have on the way the topic is treated.

4. Remind students, especially when they are reading more than one text on a topic, to note how the various texts are structured.

What I Say to Students

Earlier we talked about how we have all sorts of ingredients to consider when we are writing and how the order in which we decide to arrange those ingredients makes all the difference. Perhaps this made you think of some of the books we've been reading in our reading workshop time.

[Hold up copy of a familiar nonfiction text.]

Let's take a look at the table of contents in this book, *Oh, Rats!* by Albert Marrin.

- The Rat and I
- Rat Relatives and Ancestors
- Rats and Their Ratty Ways
- Rats and People

PURPOSE

Students learn to notice a connection between a text's structure and the meaning they glean as a result.

LESSON INTENDED FOR

- High-interest nonfiction
- Trade books
- Content area trade books
- Students at all levels

MATERIALS NEEDED

- A collection of tables of contents from a few texts on the same topic (for this lesson, I use *Oh, Rats!* by Albert Marrin and *What's Awake? Rats* by Patricia Whitehouse)

- Yummy Rats

- Pesky Rats

- Getting Rid of Rats

- Rats and Disease

- Rats to the Rescue

The way the author chose to organize information about rats is to start with the personal, then go into the history. Then, it's just about rats themselves before it moves into a bunch of chapters about how rats interact with people and vice versa.

Now, let's take a look at a different book, *What's Awake? Rats* by Patricia Whitehouse (Patricia Whitehouse, Heinemann © 2009). **This one is on the same topic, so see what this author decided to do . . .**

[Display another text's table of contents.]

- What's Awake?

- What Are Rats?

- What Do Rats Look Like?

- Where Do Rats Live?

- What Do Rats Do at Night?

- What Do Rats Eat?

- What Do Rats Sound Like?

- How Are Rats Special?

- Where Do Rats Go During the Day?

Please chat with a friend for a minute about how this author organized her book. It's about the same big topic, rats, but because of the way she organized it, you can tell it's going to cover some different things (but also some of the same things, too) from the first book.

[Listen in as students talk.]

Many of you noticed the question format. Some of you pointed out that there is less of an emphasis on rats and humans and more of an emphasis on rats just as animals.

What I hope you saw as you looked across those two different books on the same topic was that structure matters to the writer, of course, but it also matters for the reader. The way a piece is structured completely changes what information we will learn about in a particular book and what we might not ever hear about. It might also, depending on the order, affect the way we respond to the information.

For example, by starting out with mostly the negative things about rats and ending with the surprising positive things, Albert Marrin is addressing our fears before surprising us with the truth. He's sort of buttering us up.

But in the second book, it really doesn't talk about fears at all. It's more about rats in a general animal sense. I could almost imagine this same table of contents for a book about horses or giraffes. It feels more like a straight-up all-about book with the rat as the starring animal. If I didn't have any fears or concerns about rats—or even if I did—they likely wouldn't change by the time I finished Patricia Whitehouse's book. If I was reading to learn about rats, I might start with her book before going into Albert Marrin's book.

Remember, when you're reading, to note how the text you're reading is structured, especially when you are reading more than one text on a topic. It can help you plan your reading, see an author's angle, and even decide what to read next.

Trying to decide the author's angle

Writing

USING STRUCTURE TO CONVEY THE WRITER'S INTENT

PURPOSE

Students learn that writers make final decisions about text structure and sequence by knowing the most logical flow for their topic and their angle.

LESSON INTENDED FOR

- Personal expertise books
- Topic-assigned writing
- Content-specific writing

MATERIALS NEEDED

- Demonstration text—sample table of contents
- Students' drafts of their tables of contents
- Chart with examples of common logical orders for tables of contents
- Wipe-off boards or tablets with a wipe-off function (optional)

Lesson steps

1. Connect today's work to the ongoing work that students have done on structure in both their reading and writing.

2. Show a mentor example of a table of contents that follows a logical structure.

3. Share some of the more common logical structures writers use frequently.

4. Have students experiment with one or two of those options using a temporary try-it method, such as a whiteboard.

What I Say to Students

A lot of you have been realizing that when authors organize their tables of contents, it's not just a nice thing to do. It completely changes the way the information comes to the readers. A strong table of contents helps ensure that the writers' purpose for writing the texts—what they want to get across—will be covered.

Today, I want to talk about how thinking of what you want to say allows you to use a logical structure that will match that meaning. Let me show you what I mean.

If I wanted to write a book all about rats that really shows how misunderstood they are and that teaches people about some of their most useful and important attributes, then I couldn't just write a table of contents that has different kinds of rats or just an "all about" book. But I could think about a structure that could support my purpose. I could make a compare-and-contrast structure, almost like a seesaw that shows myths and truth. Or I could do a structure that is like a top-ten list, like a ranking structure, where I go from least to most amazing things about rats. Maybe I could do something like this:

There are a lot of ways to logically order tables of contents. Here are a few common ones. *[Display this chart, which you can download from the companion website.]*

Common Logical Orders for Informational Texts

- Sequential order (first, second . . .)

- Narrative (one day . . . next they . . . suddenly . . .)

- Chronological

- Topographical (from left to right, high to low)

- Ranked (least to most, best to worst, weakest to strongest, etc.)

- Kinds

- Compare and contrast

- Cause and effect

- Pros and cons

Why don't you give this a quick try on your whiteboards? Look over your current tables of contents and think, "Hey—what am I really trying to say here? And what is a nice logical way to order it?"

[Once students have finished trying out one or two and shared them with a partner, call the students back together.]

When you go off to write today, I want to challenge you to reconsider your table of contents—to revise it in a way that is logical and matches with the meaning you are after in your book.

If you are sitting there thinking, "But I love my table of contents! It is already logical and filled with meaning!" then I would like you to take a few minutes to jot down some reflections, either in the margin or in your notebook or on a sticky note. I'd like you to explain what your logical structure is and how it connects to the bigger meaning in your book. That way we can be sure we all have the best possible structures for our books.

online resources

Available for download at
**resources.corwin.com/
writersreadbetter**

VIDEO 1

In this video, I model this lesson with one of the pilot classes. I show how, as writers, the students might consider ways to structure their writing purposefully.

*resources.corwin.com/
writersreadbetter*

(Note: To read a QR code, you must have a smartphone or tablet with a camera. We recommend that you download a QR code reader app that is made specifically for your phone or tablet brand.)

Reading

INFERRING THE AUTHOR'S INTENT BY NOTICING STRUCTURE

PURPOSE

Students use the insights from the structural choices they made as writers to help them see how book authors may reveal their purpose through structure too.

LESSON INTENDED FOR

- High-interest nonfiction
- Trade books
- Textbooks
- Content area trade books

MATERIALS NEEDED

- Books that students are currently reading
- One sample table of contents you can project and annotate (in this lesson, I use *Thunderstorms* by Chana Stiefel)
- "Common Logical Orders for Informational Texts" chart (see page 31)

Lesson steps

1. Share a story about a time from real life when a building structure didn't make sense until you connected it to your personal experiences.

2. Remind students of the work they did around structure in their writing, using the chart from the lesson.

3. Guide the students through looking at the table of contents of a familiar class text, keeping in mind the moves a writer might make and trying to identify the author's intent.

4. Set students up to practice doing this with a partner, referring to the writing chart as needed.

5. Encourage students to try this with tables of contents in their independent reading—and also to notice in the future how often the writing charts can be used for reading insights.

What I Say to Students

Yesterday, I was watching my son build a building with his magnetic tiles. It was different than any other building I had seen him build. I watched and watched him build. Normally, he builds tall towers. But the building he worked on was short, only two stories, and long. It also only had walls on two sides. As I watched, I realized he was putting together various supports that would help keep the inside space as open as possible. Then, as he moved to the shelf where he keeps his toys, I realized all at once it was a garage!

I thought of us when I saw that and our lives as readers. I thought about how sometimes as readers we are confused by an author's structure. Sometimes, we don't even notice that it's different at all. But, as people who read, it is important for us to notice how the author chose to structure his or her book because it gives us an insight into a possible purpose or meaning— just like my son's new building techniques led me to realize he was building a garage for his toy cars.

Today, I want you to think about what we learned in writing and the different common logical structures that we tried out. I'd like you to take some time now to think a bit about the decisions you made, the types of structures you tried when you were writing, and what you decided to use as a structure for your piece. If you're having a hard time remembering, look back up at our chart.

[Give students time to look over their work and chat with partners.]

Now that you've considered your own structure, think about why you did what you did. I'd like you to take a minute and just jot down why you structured your piece in the way you did. How was that logical structure connected to the bigger meaning?

[Give students time to jot down their thinking.]

Now that you have your own writing in mind, let's take a look at what some authors who wrote the books we are reading did. Let's see if we can figure out the purpose of their structure, the same way I was able to figure out the purpose of my son's structure.

[Project a table of contents from a familiar text.]

Here is the contents page from *Thunderstorms* **by Chana Stiefel.**

1. Storm Brewing—How does a thunderstorm form?
2. Zap! Flash! Boom!—What is a severe thunderstorm?
3. Surviving Storms—Can people survive lightning, hail, and tornadoes?
4. Weather Watchers—How do scientists predict wild weather?
5. Run for Cover—What's the best place to be during a thunderstorm?

When I was looking at this table of contents, I noticed that the topics seem to go in an order—from what it's like right before a storm starts, through the storm itself, all the way through to what's the best place to be while there's a storm. So that makes me think that maybe the author is trying to take us on a journey—a practical journey—of thunderstorms: how we can spot them before they happen, what we should look for while they're

VIDEO 2

In this video, I model this lesson with the same class. I make the connection between what the students learned previously about crafting purposeful structures and how they can also identify these same structures in the informational texts they might read.

resources.corwin.com/ writersreadbetter

happening, and how we can keep ourselves safe. With this structure, we learn not only the scientific facts about thunderstorms but also some practical safety information.

Now, why don't you try this for a bit with the books you brought with you? With a partner, choose a book for the two of you to take a look at. See if you can name the logical structure the author was using and then see if you can use that structure to help you see her or his purpose for the book as a whole.

[Allow students time to try this strategy for a bit. Then, call them back together.]

I think many of you are already thinking this will be a fun strategy to try today in your independent reading books but also in the future.

I also want to tell you that another thing you practiced today—using the writing chart in your reading work—can be used any day to give reading insights. It is something you can try beyond today, in other situations. There are endless connections between reading and writing, and we want to try to tap into them whenever we can.

Student deep in thought over structure choices

writing

CHOOSING THE BEST PLATFORM FOR YOUR INFORMATION AND AUDIENCE

Lesson steps

1. Tell students that first drafts are perfect times to consider the way we want our pieces to look in the world and who we want to read them.

2. Explain that since they can publish digitally, they have options for both the medium and the audience.

3. Introduce the chart with a few of the digital options connected to audiences they might attract.

4. Demonstrate your own piece using a few different options from the chart.

5. Ask students to consider the platform that best matches their content and the audiences they want to reach.

6. Remind them that they can choose a different platform than the ones suggested if they know of one they like better.

What I Say to Students

Many of you are feeling ready, if not almost ready, to draft your informational pieces. So I thought today would be a good day for us to think a bit about how we want them to live in the world and who we want to read them because as we draft, we want to start to create, from the very beginning, the kind of writing we will end up with.

As you know, we have the option in this class to publish digitally. But you might not all have been thinking about the different ways that could look for informational writing. Informational writing is deeply affected by what the topic is about, as well as the audience you might have, and digital tools open up options for ways it can go as well. So you'll want to think, "Is my topic more serious? More playful? More scientific ? Is my topic more general

PURPOSE

Students study a variety of digital platforms with their topics and audiences in mind in order to decide the best way to draft their pieces digitally.

LESSON INTENDED FOR

- Personal expertise digital writing
- Topic-assigned digital writing
- Content-specific digital writing

MATERIALS NEEDED

- Student plans and rehearsals for their pieces
- "Platform and Audience Possibilities" chart (see page 36)
- A way to display options to students using demonstration writing piece (in this lesson, I use *https://padlet.com/mcolleencruz/rats)*
- Student devices

knowledge or something not everyone knows about? Do I want my audience to be kids? Grown-ups? People who already are interested in my topic or people who have never heard about it before?" There are tons of questions you can ask yourself about possible audiences and the way your topic works with those audiences.

Today, many of you will be asking yourself those questions and considering your topic and audience as you choose the platform you decide to write with. I'd like to suggest some options that might help you narrow things down a bit.

[Display the Platform and Audience Possibilities chart, which you can download from the companion website.]

online resources

Available for download at
**resources.corwin.com/
writersreadbetter**

Platform	Audience Possibilities
Multimodal article *A journalistic piece with hyperlinks, images, infographics, and other features*	• Kids interested in clicking around • Adults who love to read news • New readers who might discover the piece online
E-book *A digital version of an informational text, which may or may not use photos, sound clips, or other features*	• Kids who enjoy e-books or traditional informational books • Adults who are interested in this topic • Readers who know the writer
Podcast *An audio recording of a written informational piece. It may include more than one voice, music, or sound effects*	• Adults and kids who enjoy podcasts • Kids who want to learn more about this topic
Short documentary *A short film, based off a written script, using photos, video clips, recorded interviews, and music*	• Adults and kids who enjoy watching videos • People interested in this topic • People who might visit the website that hosts the video

Now, there are clearly more platforms than just the ones on this list. However, these cover most of the major options you might choose. For example, you might decide you want to make a website about your topic and publish a multimodal article on it, or maybe you want to make a vlog that uses a short documentary. The options go on and on.

I want to show you a few ways that my piece could go, if it was using different platforms.

[Display some samples of your work on different platforms.]

What you're going to notice as you look at each of these samples is that they are all about the same topic, rats, and that they have much of the same actual writing, only changing when the platform made it seem weird to not change some things.

[Walk them through some of the samples on the page.]

Now, writers, these are just short excerpts, not my final projects, but you can see that there are many different ways a project can work. I'd like you to take a minute to peruse your ideas and talk over your options with someone sitting near you.

[As the students speak, circulate, sometimes interjecting with options you think the students should consider while taking care not to push students toward a platform that might not work for them.]

When you go off to write today, I know a lot of you will be ready to explore platforms. You can choose from any of the ones on the chart, or you might know of another platform you'd like to try. Once you've done that, you can start thinking about any other types of rehearsal or preparation you might want to do in order to use that platform for your topic and your piece in the best way it can be used.

Reading

CONSIDERING WHY AUTHORS MIGHT CHOOSE ANALOGUE OR DIGITAL MEDIUMS

PURPOSE

Students learn to connect the choices they made as writers to the choices made by authors, particularly noticing the advantages and disadvantages of different mediums.

LESSON INTENDED FOR

- High-interest nonfiction
- Trade books
- Textbooks
- E-books
- Websites
- Blogs

MATERIALS NEEDED

- Multiple analogue copies of one book or multiple copies of several books, enough for each child or to share (in this lesson, I use a copy of the class read-aloud *The Story of Salt* by Mark Kurlansky as our model and then allow students to choose other titles during practice time)

- Digital content on the same topic as the analogue books, bookmarked or URL readily available (in this lesson I use a website from the National Park Service on the Salt Flats in Death Valley: www.nps.gov/deva/learn/nature/salt-flats.htm; I then either let the students find complementary content online or I offer a site that will work well)

Lesson steps

1. Remind students that earlier they made decisions as writers about the platforms they would use to publish their writing.

2. Explain that authors do this all the time and that, as readers of books, they want to pay attention to the form of what they read.

3. Discuss how today texts tend to come in either analogue or digital form.

4. Ask students to engage in an inquiry about the pros and cons or similarities and differences between both forms.

5. Ask students to record their discoveries on the class chart or document.

6. Reflect on how these explorations affect our reading of different materials.

What I Say to Students

Earlier we did a lot of reflecting about our topics and the mediums we think would be the best matches for our content and our audiences for the writing we're doing. And, of course, we well know that if we're thinking this way, the authors of the texts we're reading probably thought that way too. I also think it's important for us to consider not just all the different digital mediums but also the traditional paper, analogue texts as well. Nowadays, authors have the option to publish things either digitally or analogue or both. So today, I thought we should spend a bit of our reading time exploring those differences.

[Hold up the class copy of the read-aloud book.]

With partners or small groups, we will read or reread a copy of an analogue text. We're going to notice what information we get from it and the work we do as readers. Then, I want you and your fellow readers to go online and read a digital text and see what kind of information you get from that text and the kind of work you do as readers.

[Show or give students the link for the digital text.]

Once you're done discussing those two questions for both texts, I'd like you to record your findings on our class chart.

[Show students the blank What We Noticed chart, which you can download from the companion website.]

What we noticed ONLY about the analogue (paper) informational text	What we noticed about both texts	What we noticed ONLY about the digital informational text

Now remember, everything you notice does not have to be positive or negative or both. We are just trying to sort out a bit about what readers should notice when reading from these different mediums—the places where they are similar and the places where they are different.

Next, I'd like you to work with two or three other students.

[Give each group at least two copies of each analogue text and at least one suggestion of a website to pair with that topic.]

You will have ten to fifteen minutes to read the analogue text and the same amount of time for the digital. Then, I'd like you to log into the class chart and record your observations.

- "What We Noticed" chart (on this page)
- Chart paper or shared document for students to record their discoveries

online resources

Available for download at **resources.corwin.com/ writersreadbetter**

[When students are finished, bring the class together for reflection. Encourage them to look at the chart together and remove things that are repeated and add things that are missing.]

You've done a nice job with the chart. Let's take a look at it together.

[Post completed chart.]

What we noticed ONLY about the analogue (paper) informational text	What we noticed about both texts	What we noticed ONLY about the digital informational text
<ul><li>There was a lot of detail for each piece of information.</li><li>At the back of the book, there were references for where the author got the information, so it felt very trustworthy.</li><li>The text was longer, and there was more information.</li><li>Sometimes, the facts were out of date. (The tallest building has changed!)</li><li>There weren't any videos or music or things to click.</li></ul>	<ul><li>We learned information about the topic.</li><li>They both had pictures, bold print, charts, and other text features.</li><li>They had similar writing styles.</li><li>They used quotes.</li></ul>	<ul><li>There wasn't as much information.</li><li>It was hard to tell where the writer got the facts from sometimes.</li><li>There were hyperlinks that could give you more information, but you could also get distracted.</li><li>There were ads and commercials.</li><li>There were videos.</li><li>There were things to do besides read—like play games or look at pictures.</li><li>The information was very new.</li></ul>

What kind of conclusions can you draw from this? We know that authors have different purposes for different mediums. What does it make you think as readers of different mediums? Will it affect the texts you pick up and the way you approach reading them? Please work with a partner to discuss.

[Give students a few minutes to discuss. Circulate and listen in.]

A lot of you have some great ideas. Here are a few things I heard you say.

- Digital texts are good to go to for quick information or if I need to know the latest information.

- Analogue texts are good to go to if I want a deep understanding of a topic because they usually are longer and have more information.

- I feel pretty sure that if I read both a book and a website and they agree, then the facts are true.

- When I need to know a topic really well, I should be reading both paper books and digital texts.

Students use both analogue and digital tools when researching a topic.

" When many of us were students, our teachers would assign nonfiction writing, most often in the form of reports in science and social studies. I have vivid memories of my California State mission report from Miss Schmidt's fourth-grade class. Usually, the organizational aspect of the assignment was done for us via a list of information we needed to include. Some teachers even had ready-made tables of contents for us. Most of our work as informational writers was to find the facts our teacher required and then to synthesize that information by "putting it into our own words." More than one student struggled with doing the latter because often the original author's words were so logical, there were very few ways to reiterate a fact without completely destroying the syntax. "The capital of California is Sacramento" became "California's capital is Sacramento."

All of that work was tedious because students weren't able to put their own imprint on the topic in satisfying ways. When the primary task is regurgitating facts, students are not being invited to consider and try other moves that informational writers can make while drafting. The emphasis in those pieces is on the information, not on the craft of writing. Students are kept in a passive, powerless role in relation to the world's rich topics and information. **"**

PART 2
LESSONS FOR DRAFTING—AND UNDERSTANDING AUTHOR'S CRAFT

What You Will Find in This Section

Writing. These lessons focus on drafting nonfiction pieces. Whether your students are writing pieces on topics of personal expertise, something that is more research-based, or something that is content specific, this stage will help them decide for themselves the best ways to present their information to their readers. During this phase in the writing process, they will discover their piece's voice and tone. They should also be filled with enough energy and excitement for their writing to carry them through the revision process.

Reading. Meanwhile, in their nonfiction reading work, students will make connections between the choices they are making as writers and the choices professional authors make. This stage guides them to the realization that everything that shows up in an informational text was placed there by the author for a reason. The lessons in this section help students as they interact with a textbook, magazine article, online passage, or high-interest nonfiction trade book. No matter what the genre, there are people behind the texts. When students know this, they are more able to bring this same deliberateness to their own craft as writers.

When to Use These Lessons

You can use these lessons whenever they meet the needs of your students. Here are some ways to do that:

- Use the writing lessons as a supplement to your current nonfiction writing workshop unit when you feel students could use additional support or options for drafting.

- Continue to use them as part of a stand-alone unit. If you teach each one, you will guide students through the complete drafting segment of an informational piece.

- Sprinkle the lessons throughout the year, whenever your students are drafting nonfiction writing pieces and need some part of the process reinforced.

- Use them outside of writing workshop and within other disciplines, such as science and social studies, when doing reports, presentations, and so forth.

The reading work has similar flexibility. You can use the lessons to

- Continue a current informational unit or supplement one that you already teach

- Help students who are struggling with reading in their content area subjects. If that is the case, you can dip into these lessons and, with a few adjustments, teach them as part of a lesson within a subject area

- Support small-group work and extend readers of various skill levels

Preparing to Use the Lessons

There are a few things I recommend you do to prepare to teach the lessons in this chapter:

- **Offer students the choice of drafting on paper, with an app, or with another program.** When students move out of the generating and developing stage and into the drafting stage, it can help them both symbolically and practically to change materials or platforms. This step cues students that they are moving forward in the writing process. It also helps make revision easier later if students can physically or digitally cut and paste without losing original drafts. It does not matter whether the student is using paper with picture boxes, plain white loose-leaf paper, yellow drafting paper, Google Docs, Word Online, or Pages. What does matter is that students see that they are moving on in the writing process and that drafting requires a different set of muscles—a different set of tools—even though there is, of course, overlap.

- **Consider creating and using demonstration writing.** If you decide to demonstrate with your own writing in this phase of the writing process, it is wise to create a draft that you can use as a teaching tool throughout your teaching. Some teachers create one piece with anticipated teaching opportunities built in and use it again and again. Other teachers create more than one draft for different purposes. Whatever you decide to do, ultimately, the most powerful aspect for your students will be seeing your writing and the work you do on that writing so that they can hear your thought process and choices you (and they) can make as a writer.

- **Check on student progress.** You will want to keep an eye on reading volume and interest. This is the phase in the unit in which students can start to slow down after their initial excitement about a new genre or topic has lost a little of its shine. If you keep reading logs, now would be a good time for students to spend some time reflecting on how much they are reading and if certain topics, authors, or styles entice them to read more.

- **Freshen up the classroom library.** If you kept some texts out of rotation for the first part of the unit, now would be a good time to trade those books for books that have not been seen by your students in awhile.

- **Reenergize read-aloud work by bringing in a variety of texts that highlight writer's craft.** If you have a projection screen, choose a few digital multimodal texts: texts that include video, hypertext, infographics, and other features that access a variety of modalities. Look for ones that would make for good read-aloud texts and later lend themselves to lesson work. Also, consider selecting engaging trade books that highlight easily identifiable craft moves. A few are mentioned in the lessons in this part of the book, but you might want to gather a few of your own favorites as well. Finally, choose a short video or two that is informational and mirrors some of the craft moves.

As you move into these lessons, I hope that the ideas here will help you breathe new life into your students' drafts and their early stages of revision, as well as give you some new ideas (or remind you of old favorites) when it comes to considering author's craft as a reader.

Writing

DRAFTING WHAT YOU'RE MOST READY TO WRITE

PURPOSE

Students learn to draft "out of order" when that makes sense for the development of their piece.

LESSON INTENDED FOR

- Personal expertise books
- Content-specific books or reports
- Oral reports
- Students at a wide range of levels

MATERIALS NEEDED

- One of the class mentor texts (for this lesson, I use *Robots* by Melissa Stewart)
- Your demonstration draft, as described in the lesson (craft it in front of the students or prepare it ahead of time)
- Students' plans or tables of contents

Lesson steps

1. Explain to students that writers do not have to draft in order, from first chapter to last.

2. Discuss how structures, such as tables of contents and article outlines, allow writers to draft in any order they choose.

3. Demonstrate how beginning with the chapter that they feel the most expert on can help ensure that the first chapter they draft is strong.

4. Encourage students to then use that first chapter as an example to lean on as they draft subsequent chapters.

What I Say to Students

I want to let you in on a little writing secret: writers do not always draft their pieces in the order they will show up in the book. Let me show you an example.

[Hold up a copy of one of the class mentor texts.]

Melissa Stewart did not likely draft the first chapter of this book first. And this author is not alone. Since most information writers have a structure or table of contents that they are working from, they can be very free to write in whatever order they want. It's sort of like how when you have a list for the grocery store. You don't have to buy everything in order. You can go in order of what's in the aisles because the list will make sure you get everything you need.

So you might be wondering, "Hey—if I don't have to draft my first chapter or section first, how do I decide what to draft first?"

Well, of course, there are no rules, but one way that many writers find helpful is to start with the chapter on a subtopic they find easiest to write about. In my case, since I'm writing about rats, the thing I find most fascinating about them and know the most about is their bodies. I am absolutely fascinated by their bodies! Just thinking about all that information I am getting very inspired. Let me demonstrate this approach for you.

[Hold up a marker or other tool to show you are about to write.]

Let's see. I think I'll start by writing a little description about their bodies.

> Rat bodies are incredible. Since rats are mammals, they are covered in fur. It comes in different colors, depending on the type of rat: black, brown, blonde, gray, and white are common.

Hmm . . . as I was writing, I found myself starting with their fur. That was sort of surprising. But I like it. And I have so much more to say. I'll get back to this in a little bit.

What was great about this approach is that I found it super easy, and now I'm all revved up to do even more writing. But maybe even more importantly, when I'm done with drafting this chapter—and I'll be done quickly—I will have a great chapter that I can model my other chapters off of.

When you write today, I know many of you are still finishing up structuring your pieces. But a lot of you are ready to start drafting. If you are, one way you might get yourself going really quickly is by looking over your plans and deciding to start drafting today with the chapter you feel most ready to write, even if that won't necessarily be the first one in your book.

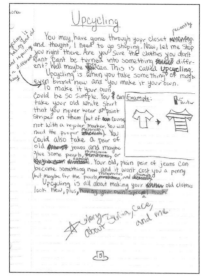

Fiona starts drafting with a chapter she feels ready to write.

Reading

SPOTTING WHAT'S MOST IMPORTANT TO AN AUTHOR

PURPOSE

Students learn to spot the sections in a book where an author might be showing off a bit, which gives them access to a window into what that author values most.

LESSON INTENDED FOR

- Reading high-interest nonfiction
- Trade books
- Articles
- Digital texts
- Students at a wide range of levels

MATERIALS NEEDED

- Your demonstration reading text (for this lesson, I use *Robots* by Melissa Stewart)
- Students' independent reading texts

Lesson steps

1. Remind students of their enthusiasm during writing and how the authors they read experience similar excitement.

2. Highlight a place in a class text where the writer makes some craft-rich moves, such as using powerful verbs and alliteration.

3. Discuss how these craft moves give readers a clue that the writer is particularly enthusiastic about this part of the topic.

4. Ask students to try to find a clue like this in a text they have already read independently. If you are in a school where students have access to digital devices, they could try this work on a digital text. However, depending how much instruction you've done in digital reading, you might want to vet the text and make sure it is either a very familiar text or a very simple one. The most important thing is that the text is accessible and also has a clear spot the students will be able to identify.

5. Remind them that this is another thing they can be on the lookout for as readers.

What I Say to Students

Earlier today we were working on our drafts, and I felt the electricity crackling in the air because so many of you chose to not only write about topics that interest you but also write today about the subtopic or chapter that interests you most.

Well, guess what, readers? Writers all have favorite parts of their manuscript, especially sentences or sections that crackle with energy. Those are great places for readers to pause and ponder. Those are often spots that are drenched in importance for the author, and therefore, they can be places of importance to us. We can often spot them because the author unloads some writing fireworks on us. When we see them, we want to take note.

Let me show you what I mean in *Robots* (Melissa Stewart, National Geographic Children's Books © 2014), the demonstration book we looked at during the writing part of this lesson. Here's a passage I want to read aloud.

[Project a page from the book and it read aloud.]

> Animals are really good at moving around on this planet. They hop across rocky cliffs. They slither and scuttle over sand. They fly and swim and tunnel underground. Many motions that animals use can also be used by robots.

Did you guys see all the fancy writing? As a writer, I was a little jealous. As a reader, I was sitting up and taking notes: now this is a place that Melissa Stewart really wants us to realize is important.

Please pull out an article from your folder, and practice looking for the spots where the author's enthusiasm shows through.

[Give the students a few minutes for this task and then bring them back together.]

As readers, you always want to keep in mind that authors help light the way to the things they value most by showing off a bit.

Trying to determine where the writer might be showing off.

Writing

STRUCTURE WITHIN SECTIONS: STACKING INFORMATION

PURPOSE

Students develop a felt sense of how writers stack information to make up drafts, and they will notice how the placement of information can be used to great effect.

LESSON INTENDED FOR

- Personal expertise books
- Content-specific books or reports
- Oral reports
- Students at a wide range of levels

MATERIALS NEEDED

- "Some Ways to Organize Information While Drafting Nonfiction Texts" chart (see page 51)
- Your demonstration text
- LEGO bricks or other connecting building blocks with various colors
- Class practice text

Lesson steps

1. Explain that when drafting sections of an informational text, writers "stack" information.

2. Share chart, "Some Ways to Organize Information While Drafting Nonfiction Texts."

3. Show them that one way to rehearse this stacking is by using a manipulative (in this case, LEGO bricks or other connecting blocks).

4. Demonstrate this with your own writing.

5. Give students an opportunity to practice this with a partner on a class text or another section of your demonstration text. If this activity is too abstract for some students, encourage them to return to other tried-and-true methods, such as making a bulleted list, creating an outline, or using a familiar graphic organizer.

What I Say to Students

One of my writing teachers once told me that writing is just building blocks and then stacking them together. When we're writing fiction, that means writing scenes and then stacking them to become stories. When we're writing essays, it means stacking ideas alongside details to support them. When it comes to information writing, I think you can guess what we might be stacking.

[Expect the students to call out a bit.]

When I am writing a chapter in my informational book, I mentally sift through all of my information that goes into that chapter, and then I think, "What might make a good order to this?" Here are a few ways an informational writer might decide to stack information.

[Show students the following chart, which you can download from the companion website.]

Some Ways to Organize Information While Drafting Nonfiction Texts

- Start with the *least* important information and end with the *most* important.

- Start with *most* important information and end with the *least*.

- Start with most surprising information and then use that to organize the rest.

- Arrange in sequential order according to steps, time, or distance.

- Mirror the organizational structure of the table of contents or shape of the whole text.

Now, that might seem like a lot of ways to try. I don't necessarily want to try all those ways, but I am curious about how my piece could go. So this is where the LEGO bricks come in. Since information writing can just be information stacked up, I can rehearse how my next chapter can go by practicing with the LEGO bricks.

Let me try the first one. This is going to be a chapter on how rats help humans. So let me just list out some of the information blocks I want to include in this chapter.

[Record your list on a chart or simply tick off the items on your fingers.]

- Can warn people when there's trouble, like when a boat is sinking

- Help with people's health because they can be used for scientific experiments

- Can sniff out explosives

- Can make excellent pets

[Hold up one LEGO brick.]

This is going to be my section about how rats can be excellent pets. I think it's interesting, but of all the things I want to include in this chapter, it's the least, so it goes first.

Available for download at **resources.corwin.com/ writersreadbetter**

VIDEO 3

I chose to film this lesson because most pilot teachers said that once they'd seen me demonstrate it, they "got it" easily. It is a lesson that sounds much more complicated on paper than it is in practice!

resources.corwin.com/ writersreadbetter

[Hold up a LEGO brick in another color.]

Now, this is going to be the warning thing—how rats let sailors know if the boat is sinking or how they let people who live near coasts know that there's going to be a flood. It's going to go next. It's a little more interesting than the pet thing but not more interesting than the rest.

[Stack that brick under the previous one. Grab a brick in a third color.]

I love the fact that there are hero rats that can sniff out explosives with their stereo-noses. So that goes next.

[Stack that brick. Hold up one more brick in a fourth color.]

Now, this last fact, the fact that rats are similar enough to humans that they can help us with scientific understandings, well, since they help so many people, that feels like the most important fact of all, so it goes on top.

[Place the stack of LEGO bricks to the side.]

Even though I liked the way that went, I want to try another possible way to organize. This time, I'm going to go with the structure that goes in the same kind of order as the table of contents.

[Continue if students would benefit from an extended demonstration. Otherwise, assign the task to them.]

Writers, why don't you try this right now with your partner. I'll hand out some cups of LEGO bricks. Think of the piece our class has been writing together and some of the information we might include in this chapter. Then, work with your partner to quickly create a few different ways the chapter might go.

[Check their groups to prompt them to try more than one way of organizing a chapter and to make sure they are on task. After students practice for a bit, bring them back together, and discuss the different options they found.]

The horse body

The horse body, just like ours, is made up of bones, they have a skeleton, with a scul, spine, rib cage, legs, along with a tale, no arms.

Pic of horse with flap of bones.

horse are at sides the that they be

eyes stattond the of horse so when eats can alert.

Their eyes can look up, down and around, whenever, and wherever. The horse also has teeth, in its upper and lower jaws. Like us humans, they have baby teeth, exept they are only repased by adult teeth, when they are worn away, from the horses way of eating. Slowly, the teeth grind down, untill they grow new teeth. The scul of a horse has to be huge to contain all the

Horse teeth

Flow diagram

teeth it has. An adult horse normally has 40 teeth, 12 incisors, 4 canines, and 12 molars. So many teeth! -that's alot of teeth!

According to Horse.

2 note to self.
new parigraph

Maggie drafts with her structure in mind.

Maggie works with a partner to experiment with building models of the ways her horse book chapters can go.

Reading

IDENTIFYING THE WAY INFORMATION IS STACKED

PURPOSE

Students use their writing experience of "stacking" to understand structure in texts they read.

LESSON INTENDED FOR

- Reading high-interest nonfiction
- Trade books
- Digital texts
- Articles
- Students at a wide range of levels

MATERIALS NEEDED

- Your demonstration reading text (ideally, a recent newspaper article)
- A class read aloud your students are familiar with
- The LEGO bricks or other connecting blocks used in the writing lesson
- "Some Ways to Organize Information While Drafting Nonfiction Texts" chart (see page 51)

Lesson steps

1. Remind students of what they did in writing workshop, and explicitly tell them it will help them as readers.

2. Refer to the chart created for the writing workshop.

3. Explain that knowing how information is stacked can help a reader; demonstrate on a news article.

4. Model by revisiting the stacking blocks and introducing the inverted triangle structure.

5. Using the class read aloud, ask students to try to identify the ways information is stacked.

What I Say to Students

Remember when we were stacking up our information for our chapters and sections in our informational pieces? Well, now we're going to take our writer selves over into our reading lives and notice how what we just did as writers is exactly what authors do. Writers organize their information into chunks and think about the best ways to arrange them. As readers, when we notice those chunks of information, it helps us understand and synthesize what we are reading. This step also helps us to think about why the author might be making those decisions.

Here is an example: I was reading an article online last night, and I noticed that the first paragraph was a whole bunch of very important information. Then, the paragraph after that was just slightly less important information.

[Project the article onto a screen, and stack representative blocks into a triangular shape or another shape while talking through the structure.]

I realized as I was reading that I was seeing exactly the structure we were talking about in writing workshop: This writer started with most important information and ended with the least.

I remembered suddenly that it was really common in journalism—so common that it even has a name: the *inverted triangle.*

[Hold up brick structure alongside the article.]

As I look at this structure, I can start to think about why the writer might have decided to organize the information in this way. Maybe she knows that a lot of people who read articles do not have a lot of time and sometimes don't finish the whole article. By writing with the most important information stacked up front, she ensures that her readers are getting informed, even if they are in a rush. And she also has set it up so that the readers who have more time will still get more information—just more like added bonus stuff, as opposed to the most necessary. The other nice thing about the writer organizing the information in this way is that if I wanted to share with someone else the most important things about this article, I could simply skim up to the top.

Let's try this by revisiting a class read aloud that we all know well. The book *Salt* by Mark Kurlansky has that great section called "How to Make Salt." Let's go back and reread the first paragraph of that section to see if we can start to think about how the author built this section.

[Project a few pages.]

> The four most common ways to find salt in nature are on the ground in dry salt beds, in the oceans, in underground springs, and in rocks under the earth.

[Flip through pages to show the pictures while talking.]

So then, remember the next paragraph is all about collecting salt by scraping it off the ground. Then, the next paragraph talked about making those salt ponds that the sun dried up. The next section is all about drilling into the underground springs. The next section is about mining for salt deep underground.

VIDEO 4

This lesson is the sister lesson to the writing lesson, giving students an opportunity to use the same manipulatives they used in their writing work in their reading. This is one of those lessons that feels especially powerful when taught after its writing component.

resources.corwin.com/ writersreadbetter

As I reread these few pages to you, I want you and your partner to see if you can identify each section and begin to think about how those different sections were placed together by the author.

[Read aloud the next section, preferably while projecting it.]

Readers, can you share what you've noticed with your partner? If it helps, you can use the LEGO bricks in front of you to demonstrate each different section that you see.

A just-built model of her chapter in her informational book

Writing

DRAFTING WITH PLACEHOLDERS FOR LATER FACTS

Lesson steps

1. Share a story about a time where research got distracting and kept you from drafting.

2. Introduce the notion of placeholders as a strategy for keeping the drafting pace fast.

3. Model doing this with a demonstration piece.

4. Give students a chance to try this in a class text or with their own writing (optional).

PURPOSE

Students learn that they can use fact placeholders to keep their momentum going.

LESSON INTENDED FOR

- Personal expertise books
- Content-specific books or reports
- Oral reports
- Research projects
- Students at a wide range of levels

MATERIALS NEEDED

- Your demonstration text
- Class practice text or students' drafts (your choice)

What I Say to Students

Writers, last night I was working on the draft of my rat book, and I am a little embarrassed to tell you that I kept getting distracted. I would start to write this chapter on the bad things rats do to humans and I would stop because I couldn't remember if it was the black plague or the bubonic plague that they were blamed for. So then I would go to my computer or start flipping through my books and get lost in all of the information. I went from learning about rats and the plague to learning about all kinds of diseases. By the time I made it back to my draft, I had completely forgotten what I was writing about! I completely messed up my flow.

I realized that I needed to take a step that a lot of information writers do all the time—that is, I needed to use placeholders so that as I'm drafting I can focus on the big picture and leave the little facts and figures to be picked up later when I am completely done with my draft. Let me show you what I mean.

[Project a blank piece of paper or a partially started draft. Begin to write.]

Rats can cause a lot of problems for humans: they can cause diseases, eat our food, and destroy our belongings.

Rats can cause a lot of diseases. For example, a long time ago.

[Stop writing and think out loud.]

Well, I think it was several hundred years ago—during medieval times. But I'm not so sure, so let me just put a line in here.

For example, a long time ago (____ years ago), people began to get very sick. Many of them died. It was the

[Stop writing and think out loud again.]

Oh—here's another spot. This was the spot that gave me trouble yesterday. I need to just put that placeholder in here again.

It was the ____ Plague. It was a horribly deadly and contagious disease.

Wow! As I'm doing this, the words are just flowing out of me. It's going so much faster than it was last night.

[Set students up to do a quick try of this strategy either using the whole-class demonstration text or with their own drafts if you feel like they could use more support.]

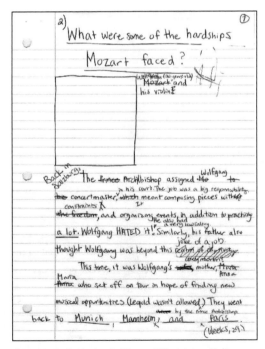

Ashley drafted with placeholders and filled them with facts later.

Reading

USING JOTS TO NOTE FACTS QUICKLY

Lesson steps

1. Model marking pages and jotting down memorable facts.

2. Ask students to work in partners to do the same.

3. Encourage them to continue this practice in their independent reading.

What I Say to Students

Earlier we were talking about how important it is to not get bogged down in locating just the right facts when we are in the flow of drafting. Now, I want to us to look at the same kind of fact overload that can occur when we are reading. I know for myself that sometimes I get so gobsmacked by one of the facts that I read that I can't seem to go forward. I want to tell everyone about it. And sometimes there are just so many facts in one juicy section that I get overwhelmed. I lose sight of even what the book is about!

I just want to remind you that we already have a trick up our sleeves to deal with exactly this sort of thing.

[Hold up a pen and the sticky note pad.]

Just like if you can't go to sleep at night because you have too many things on your mind, sometimes readers can't go forward because there are too many facts to hold onto. When I'm in this situation, I simply jot down the fact that I notice—the one that I don't want to forget but, at the same time, want out of my mind. So here. On this page in *No Monkeys, No Chocolate*, there's a fact about the maggots eating the coffin ants' brains.

[Project excerpt of text.]

While the hardworking ants slice up the leaves and carry the pieces back to their nest, female coffin flies land on the ants and lay eggs inside their heads.

PURPOSE

Students learn that instead of getting overwhelmed by trying to retain all facts as they read, they can jot down things that attract their attention and continue their regular reading pace.

LESSON INTENDED FOR

- Reading high-interest nonfiction
- Trade books
- Articles
- Digital texts (if students have access to digital or analogue annotation tools)
- Students at a wide range of levels (however, best for students who are reading above a guided reading level K)

MATERIALS NEEDED

- Your demonstration reading text
- A class read aloud that your students are familiar with, with a place chosen that is filled with facts (in this lesson, I use Melissa Stewart's *No Monkeys, No Chocolate* and Greg Pizzoli's *The Impossibly True Story of Tricky Vic: The Man Who Sold the Eiffel Tower*)

- A giant sticky note pad, chart paper with large yellow squares drawn to look like sticky notes, or a reading notebook for demonstration
- Sticky notes, reading notebooks, or scraps of paper for each student to write on

When the eggs hatch, tiny maggots wriggle out and eat the ants' brains.

I can now mark that page and jot on my sticky note the fact that I don't want to forget.

Later on, I can look over those facts and remember what attracted me to those spots in the text. Or else, I can put all the facts together and grow ideas for writing.

Why don't you try this with an excerpt from another class read aloud?

[Project an excerpt or hand out copies for partners to look at.]

With your partner, reread the paragraph I boxed out. It is chock-full of facts. If any catch your eye, can you and your partner do a quick jot? Then, talk about what and why you decided to jot.

[As students read and talk with their partners, circulate and remind them to simply jot the facts they find worth remembering.]

Now that you've had some practice, please remember that you can also use this approach during your independent reading.

Students jotting and talking while reading

writing

TAKING A DRAFT BREAK
TO RESEARCH

Lesson steps

1. Explain that professional writers take breaks from their drafting for many reasons.

2. Give some examples of ways that authors take breaks.

3. Model how to make a plan for the break.

4. Ask students to make their own plan for the break.

What I Say to Students

Over the past couple of days, I know you have been drafting your hands off! As you inch closer and closer to finishing your draft, I want to let you in on a little secret: professional writers often take breaks from their drafting.

Writers do this for a whole lot of reasons. Probably first and foremost, it's because writing can be hard work, and sometimes, you need a breather. Or sometimes, you're stuck on the direction you want to go, and the break allows you to get a fresh perspective and reenergize.

Breaks can happen all kinds of ways. Some writers clean the refrigerator and daydream about their writing while they are doing it. Some take a walk and think. With nonfiction drafting, we can take breaks to research. Maybe we skim some books we've read to pick up techniques we might use, find new texts, jump online to do a quick Internet search, reread our notes from research we've already done . . . all good breathers. Remember how we recently talked about using placeholders for facts we don't yet know when we don't want to stop our writing flow to work on them? Well, if you decide to take a break for research, you can use that time to go and fill in those gaps.

PURPOSE

Students practice taking breaks while drafting to research.

LESSON INTENDED FOR

- Personal expertise books
- Content-specific books or reports
- Oral reports
- Research projects
- Digital projects
- Students at a wide range of levels (*Note:* Students whose current reading levels reduce the number of classroom texts available to them might need an alternate lesson.)

MATERIALS NEEDED

- Your demonstration text
- A text, digital or analogue, that can be used to model research of your demonstration topic

Let me try this with my piece.

[Pull out a piece to demonstrate.]

First I need to make a plan—I don't want this break to take more than twenty minutes. So I think the first step in my plan is to answer some of the questions my friends had about this chapter on rat bodies when I shared it with them the other day. I don't know if I'll include the information in the final piece, but it might be really interesting, and I might decide I want to include it. Then, after that, I can go back and reread my notes from my reading notebook to see if there are any facts or ideas I haven't yet included in my draft that I should include. Let me just jot down my research plan.

[Record notes visibly on your research plan.]

1. Answer my friends' questions.

2. Reread my reading notebook for overlooked facts and ideas.

3. If time, skim through one of the books I haven't spent as much time with.

So writers, before you leave the meeting area today, please jot down your plan for when or if you decide to take a research break.

Researching into a draft is sometimes messy.

Reading

NOTICING THE VARIOUS WAYS AUTHORS USE QUOTATION MARKS

Lesson steps

1. Explain that the focus for the lesson will be the different ways authors use quotation marks.

2. Ask students to work together to identify sections from a shared text with quotation marks.

3. Encourage students to decide why the authors chose to use these marks.

4. Complete a chart together that explores the author's use of quotation marks.

What I Say to Students

A lot of us, while taking breaks in our drafting, have been revisiting texts we read a few weeks ago. This time, we've been noticing things we hadn't really noticed before, such as how different authors use punctuation to help highlight their facts. Sometimes, authors list facts in bullet form or in margin boxes. Sometimes, they just state their facts. Today, we are going to focus on quotation marks. We are going to work in teams to reread a section from our class read aloud.

You and your team can decide what section you want to reread. While you're rereading, look for quotation marks. When you spot them, copy that section down. Then, work with your team to theorize why the author used quotation marks in that way for that particular section of text.

Try to imagine possible reasons for the choices the author made. If you were the author of this piece, why might you have made this decision? As you work, I will stop by your group to see how you're doing. Then, we'll meet as a class again to discuss what we've noticed and chart our ideas.

PURPOSE

Students are guided through an inquiry to see the different ways authors use quotation marks in informational text— and why it's important to notice these differences.

LESSON INTENDED FOR

- Reading high-interest nonfiction
- Trade books
- Articles
- Digital texts
- Students at a wide range of levels (*Note:* Texts that directly quote sources are more challenging to find below a guided reading level M.)

MATERIALS NEEDED

- A text that the students can practice on during the lesson— ideally, one copy per student of a familiar excerpt from a class read-aloud text (the piece should demonstrate a variety of ways to use quotation marks; for this lesson, I use *Oh, Rats!* by Albert Marrin)
- Chart to analyze an author's use of quotation marks (see page 64, which contains a chart inspired by the work Katie Ray [1999] did around mentor texts in the writing workshop; students will fill in the fourth column, which is for writing, later as part of writing workshop)

[When the students complete their inquiry, display the blank Quotation Marks chart, which you can download from the companion website.]

Section of text using quotation marks	What we think that section means	Why we think the author used quotations in this way	Ways we could use it in our own writing

[Discuss the students' findings and then complete the chart together.]

Completed chart exploring the author's use of quotation marks

Students discuss craft they noticed in the text.

writing

DRAFTING WITH AN AUDIENCE IN MIND

Lesson steps

1. Explain to students that they will watch a video clip of someone teaching. Ask them to watch the way the presenter presents the content.

2. Show excerpt of the teaching video.

3. Ask students to discuss what they noticed about the way the presenter presented the content.

4. Give students a copy of a written text, teaching about the same content as the video.

5. Ask students to compare the two texts.

6. Explain that one reason the texts are different is because of the audiences.

7. Show excerpts of demonstration writing—two different versions of the same topic, written for different audiences.

8. Remind students to consider their audiences as they draft.

What I Say to Students

We're going to start today by watching a very quick video clip where someone is trying to teach you something. I want you to notice how the speaker presents the content.

[Show an excerpt of a speech or lecture; in this case, I recommend a 2–3 minute segment of Sophie Scott's TED Talk, "Why We Laugh."]

Writers, can you quickly talk with someone sitting near you about what you just learned about and what you noticed about how the writer—that is, the speaker—presented the content?

[Once students have finished talking, share a piece of text written on the same topic as the oral text. Project it, or hand out a copy of it. I suggest using the article "Does Laughing Help You Live Longer?"]

PURPOSE

Students learn to envision the precise audience for their piece, and they discover how doing so can help them make decisions about tone, structure, and information.

LESSON INTENDED FOR

- Personal expertise books
- Content-specific books or reports
- Oral reports
- Research projects
- Digital projects
- Students at a wide range of levels

MATERIALS NEEDED

- Your demonstration text, with different versions for different audiences on hand
- A clip of a TED talk or similar recorded lecture (I recommend an excerpt from Sophie Scott's TED talk, "Why We Laugh")
- A published text that complements the recorded lecture, such as "Does Laughing Help You Live Longer?"
- Student drafts

Now, writers, you have probably noticed right away that the text I just gave you is on almost the same topic as the one we watched on the video. This time, when you talk with your partner, I'd like you to talk about the written text and compare it with the video. If you finish talking about that, you might begin to talk about why you think those similarities and differences might exist.

[Listen in on student conversations. Then, pull the class back together when the conversations start to die down.]

One of the biggest influences on a writer's work is the person or people who will be reading and experiencing the writing. For example, we just studied two texts that were about the same topic. But because the audiences—and the way the audiences receive the information—are different, it shouldn't be too much of a surprise to see lots of things were actually presented differently.

Of course, it's not just video and written texts that are different because they have different audiences. Most texts, such as other written texts on this same topic, will be completely different because of the different audiences the authors are writing for.

Let me show you the piece I am writing.

[Project the latest version of your demonstration text.]

> Rats have complex relationships. They have their immediate family, just like we do. That includes parents and offspring. They also have extended family, with aunts, uncles, cousins, and grandparents. These extended families become part of a larger group that is called a *clan*.

This text is really written for students who are in the same grade as you. But if I were to write this for little kids—like kindergartners—I would need to do lots of things differently. I would need to simplify the language; I would need to add a lot more pictures. I would need to take out some of the more disturbing facts that come later in my piece. And if I were to write it as a formal piece for people who have more scientific expertise, I wouldn't need to explain some of the science terms, and I could go deeper into some of the tiny details. Let me show you what that could look like.

[Project different versions of the main text, talking through the ways they are different.]

> Do you have a family? Most people do. They are made up of the grown-ups who care for us, usually our parents, and the children. Rats are like people. They have families too!

> Rats, like most mammals, have complex social and familial structures. At their center is a family humans might describe as nuclear. This

frequently, although not always, involves a mother and a father rat, depending on the species, in a long-term relationship that involves coparenting the offspring.

Today, when you are working on your draft, think about who is your audience. Who do you imagine reading your piece? What are things you'll include and ways you'll write because of the audience you have in mind?

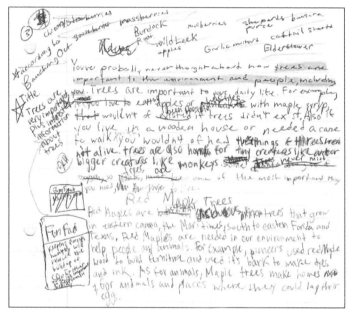

Brianna drafts her piece with readers who want to know more about trees in mind.

Reviewing a draft with specific readers in mind

Reading

NOTICING THE DIFFERENT GENRES OF VARIOUS PUBLICATIONS ON THE SAME TOPIC

PURPOSE

Students make a connection between how they consider their audience as they write and how the authors they read make similar choices about reaching their audiences.

LESSON INTENDED FOR

- Reading high-interest nonfiction
- Trade books
- Articles
- Digital texts
- Students at a wide range of levels

MATERIALS NEEDED

- A few text sets on a topic that's familiar to students but in different forms and at different levels of accessibility to help illustrate how the same topic can be treated uniquely by different authors (e.g., a set might include articles, a graphic informational book, a photo essay, and a few different nonfiction books; for this lesson, I use *Roald Dahl's Revolting Recipes*, *Boy*, and *Going Solo* by Roald Dahl and *The War in the Air* by Gavin Lyall—although any general nonfiction book on World War II Royal Air Force will do.)

Lesson steps

1. Explain how purpose often affects what type of texts we turn to.

2. Ask students to choose between two different types of texts to best match a certain purpose.

3. Explain that both texts might be good choices, particularly if read together.

4. Offer students different texts organized around a central topic yet ranging widely in terms of tone, focus, and readability. Encourage students to read from a wide range of text types to broaden their base of knowledge.

What I Say to Students

The other day, my son wanted to know how many justices are on the Supreme Court. I was pretty sure I knew the answer, but I wasn't 100 percent sure. So I hopped on the Internet, and with my son, we looked up the answer, reading a short article on the topic. But that got me thinking about how if he had asked me a different question—like if he wanted to know more about the life of one of the justices, say Ruth Bader Ginsberg—he could do a quick Internet search, but it would probably be better if he read a biography on her. And depending on how much he wanted to know, he might want to read different types of biographies.

As readers, we can learn from lots of different types of nonfiction texts, but depending on our purposes, we should consider what types of texts we want to turn to. I have here a short stack of texts. There are some articles, a graphic informational book, a photo essay, and a few different nonfiction books—some with lots of pictures and some with hardly any at all. When I am reading nonfiction, particularly if I am reading about a particular topic I want to know more about, I want to consider the different forms. And not only that, I want to consider the different kinds of information the different forms can give me. For example, if I really want to get some visual information, then a photo essay, a nonfiction book with lots of pictures, or an image search on the Internet will all be helpful. If, however, I want to get into the real technical nitty-gritty of a topic, I probably want to read a dense and serious book on the topic—probably with few (if any) pictures.

Let's try this together now.

[Hold up two texts on a topic the students are familiar with.]

If I wanted to learn more about Roald Dahl's life, should I read this *Revolting Recipes* cookbook based on all the food in his books, or should I read *Boy*, a memoir he wrote about his childhood? Please hold up one thumb for the first book or two thumbs for the second book.

[Pause for voting.]

If I wanted to know more about what life was like for Roald Dahl when he was a pilot during World War II, then should I read his autobiography that talks about his life during wartime, or should I read this nonfiction book about the Royal Air Force, which Dahl was a part of during World War II?

[If students choose the autobiography, which is likely, point out that both sources are actually good choices—especially if read together.]

I think you are getting a hang of this. I can tell that some of you are already thinking about the books waiting for you back at your seats and wondering which ones to begin with. I've left you some texts that are organized around a central topic yet range widely in terms of tone, focus, and readability. You can also choose to read from your independent materials.

Before you go, it's important to keep in mind that not everyone uses the same text for the same reasons. And some of us might find a few go-to texts that we use for almost everything we need. But it's also helpful as nonfiction readers to know that if we want to broaden our knowledge base, it's a very good idea to read widely, in many different forms.

Reading from a wide variety of texts and genres on the same subject

writing

DRAFTING IN A MOOD OR TONE THAT MATCHES THE CONTENT

Lesson steps

1. Ask students to watch a serious commercial to identify the topic, tone, and mood.

2. Work with students to fill in a chart to share what they noticed.

3. Show them a second video with a very different tone and content, and ask them to repeat the exercise. Complete the chart together.

4. Point out that a lot of authors try to match the mood of their piece to the kind of information they're presenting and with the topic itself.

5. Ask students to try this approach by writing a quick paragraph about a familiar topic.

What I Say to Students

Last night I was sitting on the couch, getting ready to watch my favorite cooking show, when I saw two commercials back to back. As I was watching them, I noticed a relationship between the content—or topic—and the way the information was presented—the tone. Let me show you the first one. As you watch, see if you can name the topic and also the tone and mood of the commercial. You might even begin to think of why the people who made the commercial might have made a decision to create that mood or tone.

[Show a commercial that is very serious in tone but wouldn't be scary to children.]

Let's just do a quick jot of what we noticed in terms of content and tone or mood and some of the thoughts you have about why the authors might have made those decisions.

PURPOSE

Students learn to craft a mood or tone that is a good match for the angle they are taking with their topic. *Note: Because this writing lesson is so interconnected to the reading lesson that follows, you might want to include the reading lesson as a connected part of your writing workshop. You could, alternately, blend the two sessions together.*

LESSON INTENDED FOR

- Personal expertise books
- Content-specific books or reports (if students have choice in form)
- Oral reports
- Research projects (if students have choice in form)
- Students at a wide range of levels

MATERIALS NEEDED

- Your demonstration text
- A couple of short video clips, such as commercials, that show different tones for different topics (for this lesson, I chose a bullying prevention ad from the Ad Council "I Am a Witness" and the "Discover the Forest" video from the Ad Council)
- Students' drafts
- Whiteboards or slates

[Working with students, fill in a chart such as the following.]

Topic	Tone/Mood	Reasons why
Bullying	• Serious • Dark • A little dangerous • Ideas clearly communicated • Uses a small moment to help share information	• It's a serious topic • To make sure people took it seriously (not everyone takes bullying seriously)

Now, let's watch this second video. Let's do that same work. Let's look for the topic and the mood or tone. Let's also begin to build a theory about why the commercial makers might have created the commercial that way.

[Show a second video with a very different tone, as well as a very different topic, to help make a strong contrast.]

As you're talking to your partner, consider what we want to add to our chart.

[When they are finished talking, return to the chart and continue to fill it out together.]

Topic	Mood/Tone	Reasons why
Bullying	• Serious • Dark • A little dangerous • Ideas clearly communicated • Uses a small moment to help share information	• It's a serious topic • To make sure people took it seriously (not everyone takes bullying seriously)
Nature appreciation	• Silly • Bright • Fun • Uses a small moment • Uses clear language	• It's a topic about enjoyment and fun • It's trying to convince people to see the forest as fun, so it's a fun commercial

Great—so what we're seeing, I think you'll agree—is that a lot of authors try to match the mood of their piece to the kind of information they're presenting and with the topic itself. So let's try this ourselves right now. On your whiteboard, please write a little paragraph, a sort of quick try, for a piece on littering in the school yard—something we've talked a lot about. What should people know? What tone should you use?

[After students have tried this out on their whiteboards, ask them to hold up their tries. Note students whose tone seems to match the topic of their writing and those where it could use more tweaking. Encourage the students to give feedback to each other, or plan to meet with students who want or need more work on this later.]

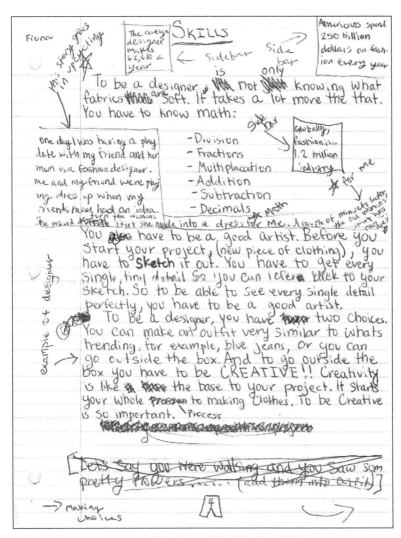

Fiona aims for a conversational and friendly tone while writing about fashion.

Reading

NOTICING WHEN THE TONE DOESN'T MATCH THE TOPIC

PURPOSE

Students learn to pay attention to the connection between the tone and the topic and to identify any lack of match as a signal for the reader to pay close attention and determine *why*.

LESSON INTENDED FOR

- Reading high-interest nonfiction
- Trade books
- Articles
- Digital texts
- Content area reading
- Students at a wide range of levels

MATERIALS NEEDED

- A few texts—each on a different topic, with a different tone (for this lesson, I use *That's Gross!* by Crispin Boyer, *Inside Earthquakes* by Melissa Stewart, and *When Is a Planet Not a Planet?* by Elaine Scott)
- An additional text on one of those topics but with a very different tone (for this lesson, I use *Pluto's Secret* by Margaret Weitekamp and Diane Kidd)

Lesson steps

1. Explain that writers often select a tone that matches their topic.

2. Use different texts on similar subjects to show that this can be handled in alternate ways.

3. Ask students to work with a partner to explore how different tones can work for different purposes.

What I Say to Students

Readers, I'm going to keep this quick, because so much of what I want to say about reading today connects so tightly with what we were talking about with writing. That is, we know that authors often make decisions about the tone of their writing based on their topic. For example, look at this book on earthquakes, *Inside Earthquakes* by Melissa Stewart.

[Hold up book on a serious topic that has a cover with a very serious tone.]

Just by looking at the title and cover photo, we can tell this is a very serious book. Earthquakes are no laughing matter.

But this book, *That's Gross*, has a silly font, pictures of people picking their noses, and pictures of skunks. I can tell that it has a very silly tone, in part because gross things are fun to talk about.

Now, before I hold up the next book, I want you to think about what tone this next book might have. What might its cover look like? What might its tone be like? It's a book on planets—in particular, it's about Pluto, which used to be classified as the ninth planet in our solar system but has now been reclassified as a dwarf planet. Turn and talk to your partner.

[Give students time to discuss what possible tone the book might have.]

Let me show you one of the books I have on Pluto, *When Is a Planet Not a Planet? The Story of Pluto.* Give a thumbs up if this book appears to match the style you were predicting. I'll show you a few of the inside pages too so you can get a real sense of it.

[Display the book.]

But here's the thing—this is not my only book about Pluto. Here's another one. Before I show it to you, I want to say that when I saw this book, I was a little surprised at first, but I later understood why the author used this tone. Here's *Pluto's Secret.* Do you notice how different it looks from the first book? This one has a little cartoon Pluto, which is making sort of a smug face, and bubble letters on the title. The first book had all sorts of serious images from space—real photographs and a very serious font for lettering the title. Can you tell your partner what you think about that? Why might two different authors use completely different tones when writing about the same topic?

[After students have chatted for a bit, bring them back together.]

Today, readers, I want you to be on the lookout for the author's tone. How does the author you are reading craft his or her piece? Does it match the topic? Is it somewhat surprising? When it's surprising, think about why the author might have made that decision and how it might affect the way you take in information about that topic.

Reading alongside a partner to explore the author's use of tone.

Writing

DRAFTING TO SOMEONE ELSE'S SPECIFICATIONS

PURPOSE

Students learn that in school and in the publishing world, authors must sometimes adhere to guidelines. *Note: This lesson is meant to be a bridge lesson for students who are used to writing in a workshop style but who need to follow a certain set of guidelines. This is a good lesson to use if you are working within a content area or with another teacher to help students understand why guidelines can be important.*

LESSON INTENDED FOR

- Content-specific books or reports
- Oral reports
- Research projects in a particular subject area
- Students at a wide range of levels

MATERIALS NEEDED

- Any guidelines you want students to meet for their class project
- Author guidelines for book publishers, journals, or websites

Lesson steps

1. Explain that professional writers must often follow guidelines.

2. Share a few sets of author guidelines.

3. Review your class submission guidelines with the students.

4. Leave plenty of time for questions and discussion.

What I Say to Students

Today, writers, I want to just have a quick meeting to make sure we are all clear on what our expectations are for this project. Even though we are doing this piece in writing workshop, there are also certain pieces of information we need to cover in our subject area.

Just like your teachers sometimes give you writing guidelines for school projects, professional writers also get guidelines from their publishers. Let me show you a few examples.

[Project guidelines for a professional publication.]

Do you notice how this includes all sorts of things—from the topics that are acceptable, the amount of research expected, and even how many words the submission can be? Professional publications do this because they each have their own house style and content requirements, which means requirements that are specific to their magazine. The content specifications ensure that readers will know what to expect when they pick up their publication.

Teachers do the same thing. Their house style is what they require in their class. Let's look at our class submission guidelines. I will highlight the parts that are most important. These might mean more to you now than they did when we first announced this project because you are now in the midst of drafting and have a pretty good idea of how you want your piece to go.

[Leave plenty of time for discussion and questions.]

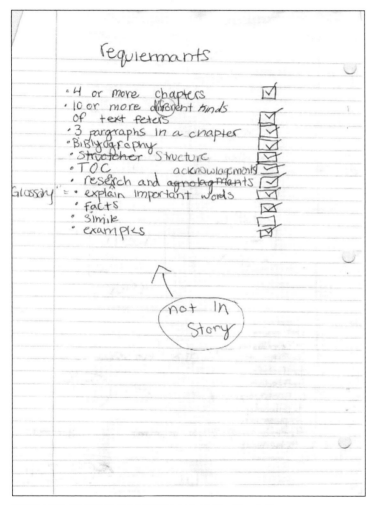

Maggie writes out her personal guidelines on the inside of her draft.

Reading
NOTICING A PUBLISHER'S APPROACH

PURPOSE

Students learn to be on the lookout for the signature characteristics of a particular series or author or publisher and to consider how those characteristics influence their reading expectations.

LESSON INTENDED FOR

- Reading high-interest nonfiction
- Trade books
- Articles
- Digital texts
- Textbooks
- Whole-class study on same content
- Students at a wide range of levels

MATERIALS NEEDED

- A text set by the same author (these do not need to be on the same topic)
- A text set by the same publisher (these do not need to be on the same topic)

Lesson steps

1. Explain how readers often have specific expectations from different publishers, just as consumers have different expectations from different vendors.

2. Review a familiar book series or author together (my favorites include *National Geographic, True Books, DK Readers*, and anything by Melissa Stewart; for this lesson, I use three books from the *National Geographic for Kids* imprint: *Robots* by Melissa Stewart, *Volcanoes* by Ann Schreiber, and *Bears* by Elizabeth Carney).

3. Guide students to consider what they might expect in an unfamiliar book by using what they know from another.

What I Say to Students

Yesterday, I was having a conversation with Nico. He was telling me his plans for reading the books in his stack. All of his books were from the same publisher, *National Geographic for Kids*. Before he even opened up the next book, he was already setting up his sticky notes. This is what he said to me.

> I just know that this book will have a table of contents that will help me divide my learning into sections. I know it will feature some new vocabulary words, so I want to get a collection spot going. I know it will have text features that will have extra information that won't be included in the main part of the text, so I need to be prepared to think about how that information fits.

Wow! That's a lot to expect. And he's probably right. But it also makes me realize that there are a lot of things in life like that, aren't there? **Like when we watch a television series, even though each show is different, we** start to expect certain things from each episode. Or when we play a video game from the same franchise, like the Mario Brothers, we start to expect things to go a certain way. And now that I'm thinking about it, I have noticed the same is true with certain musicians and actors too! I'm sure there are certain things we could expect not just from certain publishers and series but also certain authors. For instance, whenever I read a Seymour Simon book, I expect beautiful pictures.

Let's take a look at a few books I have up here and try it. Let's look at a familiar book series or author and think about what we might expect in the next book by using what we know from the other.

[I hold up a familiar book and display it on the document camera.]

You remember this book, *Robots? [I flip few a through pages, reading through the table of contents and a page or two.]* Remember how this book starts with a lot of background information about the topic? In this case, robots? And then it moves into more specific information, including examples, using fun facts, captions, and a glossary.

Now, if we go into this next book, which we haven't read as a class, but we know it's by the same publisher or imprint, we can look at the topic, hold in our minds how the last book we read from this series went, and then anticipate how this new book will go. So if the next book that we look at is also in the same series, but this one is called *Volcanoes*, we can hold in our minds the idea that the first part of the book is going to start with a lot of background information, then there will be more and more specific information. Then, we expect that there might be some fun facts, captions, and a glossary. Let's read and find out.

[Display the book, confirming predictions that were accurate and adjusting for anything that was different.]

Let's try it one more time with one more book, so we can see how much our reading in this series experience is similar, but this time, I'm not going to say a thing. I want you and the people who are sitting with you to make some predictions. How is this next book going to go? It's called *Bears*, and it's by Elizabeth Carney.

[Listen as students discuss, prompting them to consider the last two books if needed]

So even though this book was on a completely different topic—it was nothing like robots or volcanos—the way the book was written still had something in common with those other two books. So our brains could stop and notice those things and not have to learn new structures. Instead, our brains could think a bit more deeply about the content. This is something for us to remember whenever we choose to read a book that is by a familiar author or from a familiar series. We should keep that in mind as we read, we can use what we know from other books like that one to help us read to anticipate what the next book will be like.

Reading closely across a few books from the same publisher and comparing as she goes

Writing

FACT-CHECKING DIGITAL INFORMATION FOR ACCURACY

Lesson steps

1. Ask students, "What are the most important jobs of an informational writer?"

2. Reflect on their comments, and either underline or suggest the role of ethical fact usage when writing anything.

3. Explain that this fact-checking is always important, but that it is especially important in digital publications because erroneous information can spread like wildfire in the online world.

4. Introduce the chart.

5. Demonstrate drafting a sentence with a focus on checking to make sure the information is accurate.

6. Encourage students to do the same.

7. Suggest that students act as fact-checkers for each other's pieces.

PURPOSE

Students learn that fact-checking and usage is one of the most important jobs of a digital informational writer.

LESSON INTENDED FOR

- Personal expertise digital writing
- Topic-assigned digital writing
- Content-specific digital writing

MATERIALS NEEDED

- A digital device to use for fact-checking
- A sentence or two from your demonstration piece to use to demonstrate fact-checking
- "Digital Information Writers Take Responsibility for the Facts in Their Pieces" chart (see page 82)

What I Say to Students

I'd like to start our writing time together by asking you a question. "What is the most important job of an informational writer?" Please discuss this with people sitting around you.

[Listen in. Then, pull the group back together.]

I hear people talk about making the writing exciting or interesting for readers or using great vocabulary. All very important things. However, I would say the single most important thing writers of informational texts need to focus on is to make sure that every fact they use really and truly is a fact. In other words, we don't want to be writing things we aren't 100 percent sure are true, or worse, things we are pretty sure are not right.

This is always true for informational writers. But it becomes especially true when you publish digitally. One reason is that when you publish digitally, you can't be sure who will read your piece and whether or not you can explain yourself. Digital pieces can go viral, and if the information is wrong, tons of people can go around thinking something that is not true is true.

[Pause to let the gravity sink in.]

The digital information writer's first responsibility then is to make sure every fact included in his or her writing is true. Here are some steps we can take as we're drafting to make sure that we are acting like responsible writers.

[Display this chart, which you can download from the companion website.]

Digital Information Writers Take Responsibility for the Facts in Their Pieces

Step 1. As we draft, we ask ourselves before we write something down, "Am I sure this is a fact?"

Step 2. If we're not sure if a fact is true, we double-check by doing a book or an Internet search, making sure there is backup in at least two places. We might even call or e-mail an expert in the field to verify its accuracy.

Step 3. If we cannot find sources that agree with that "fact," we do not include it.

Step 4. When we are done drafting, we ask a fact-checker to double-check our facts.

I'm going to try a bit of that right now.

[Start to draft in front of the students. Choose something that is based on speculation versus fact.]

RATS LIKE TO HAVE FUN.

Hmm. Well, I have to ask myself, "Am I 100 percent sure about that?" Because I want to write about how rats tickle each other. I am guessing that they have fun, because I think tickling is fun. But do I know for sure rats have fun? I better look it up.

[Model doing a quick Internet search. Show the responses on the screen.]

Okay. So I don't see anything that says that. I need to change my wording then.

[Pause and update your draft.]

Rats like to have fun—seem like they like to have fun. That is
because they have been seen tickling each other.

I want to check that second sentence, too. So I think you get what I'm doing there. Now, I want you to notice that this is important to do all the way through your drafting. Using Internet search tools can make it easier and faster, but you can double-check books as well.

When I am all done with my draft, I can ask friends if they would be willing to swap with me and we can be fact-checkers for each other's pieces.

When you are writing today, I'd like you to check back on this chart and see how you're doing with your responsibilities as a digital writer of informational texts. Then, when you're done with your draft, if not today, but someday soon, I'd like you to seriously consider asking a friend to fact-check your work, just to be doubly sure.

Fact-checking takes serious concentration.

Reading

IDENTIFYING FALSE INFORMATION

PURPOSE

Students learn some steps to take when reading in order to better identify reliable and unreliable sources.

LESSON INTENDED FOR

- Websites
- Blogs
- Other Internet sites

MATERIALS NEEDED

- "Some Strategies for Spotting Source Reliability" chart (on page 85)
- A website from a reliable source your students might be familiar with (e.g., *Time for Kids* or *National Geographic for Kids*)
- A website from a reliable source your students are not likely to be familiar with (e.g., The Smithsonian, The Museum of Natural History, or a kid-friendly mainstream news source)
- A website from a nonreliable source (e.g., "Jennifer Aniston Did WHAT To Her Hair?" from Stylecaster or All About Explorers)

Lesson steps

1. Explain to students that although they were very careful as writers to make sure their facts were accurate, not all writers and editors publishing online are as responsible with verifying the information in their pieces.

2. Tell students that some of the information is mistaken and some is intentionally untrue. As readers, they need to be on alert for what is reliable and what is not.

3. Introduce steps for identifying reliable sources, using the chart to help.

4. Ask students to explore a few bookmarked websites in small groups, using the chart or other steps to help them identify whether the texts are reliable or not.

5. After their exploration, debrief with students to discuss how this experience will affect their reading in the future.

What I Say to Students

Remember how we talked earlier, in writing workshop, about how incredibly important it is, as ethical digital, informational writers, to make sure our facts are absolutely accurate? Well, guess what? There are actually writers who do not put that kind of care into the facts that they use. Sometimes by accident. Sometimes on purpose. As digital readers, we need to make sure that when we're reading information, we are not being fooled by false facts.

When I am reading, there are several things I do to make sure I don't get fooled and that the information I am reading is accurate. Let's look at this chart.

[Display the chart, which you can download from the companion website.]

Some Strategies for Spotting Source Reliability (aka: Is This News Fake?)

- Look for a trusted and familiar source to start.

- Check the authors, and see what their backgrounds are.

- Find the date published to make sure it's recent.

- Check to see if the story appears in two or more sources (ideally, sources with different audiences).

- Count the experts and references in the article. Ideally, there should be at least two sources of information cited, if not more.

- Ask yourself, "Does this fit with what I know? Does it seem realistic?"

Available for download at **resources.corwin.com/ writersreadbetter**

Now, at first glance, the things you can do to spot reliable (or not reliable) sources seem very easy. But just to make sure we're practicing this to make sure we really have it, I have bookmarked three websites for you to check out. I'm going to ask you to work in teams and see if you can determine if each source is reliable or not, using our strategies.

[Guide the students to find the bookmarked sites. Coach them to use the strategies for identifying the source reliability, asking them questions and encouraging them to back up information using additional resources or to refer to the strategies on the chart. Then, call them back together.]

As you were reading and talking, I noticed a lot of you found yourself moving out of the article and doing some other online searching to back up facts found in the articles you were originally reading. This is such a good move! I also noticed that you often grew more suspicious and more likely to do this move when the information in the article felt particularly shocking. I think that's a great instinct. The big idea from this lesson is not that one particular article is fake or real or reliable or unreliable but that you need to have an awareness and a suspicion of the things you read online, knowing that you are developing the skills you need in order to identify the reliability of the sources you are reading.

Close to the end of a project, fact-checking from multiple sources becomes more important.

All writers have a favorite part of the process. For many it is the beginning stage, when they are just tossing ideas around in their head. For others, it's when they put pen to paper or fingers to keyboard, and they can see the endless possibilities take shape. Still others most relish the cleanup stage of editing. My favorite part is revision, which has always been the carrot at the end of my proverbial writing stick. I slog through the other parts, knowing that at the end of developing and drafting, I will be able to revise. During revision, I fill in any holes, match my vision with the words, and make all of the components as smooth and as close to my intentions as possible.

So imagine my shock when I discovered how many of my students hated revision. They loathed it. I was further shocked when I realized that students had very similar feelings around rereading a book or an article for deep analysis and possible critique.

What was going on? I got curious, and I theorized that the students' aversion to either kind of revisiting was springing from the same place psychologically. Both revision and analysis were making kids feel diminished. Many students believe that when writers must revise or readers must reread in order to analyze, they did something wrong in the first place, and now they must fix it. To combat this misunderstanding, I try to make this work as filled with high energy and as engaging as possible. I bust out the enticing supplies like snazzy pens and different sized or shaped sticky notes. I also try to challenge myself as a teacher and as a reader and writer so that students see revision and analysis as they should see it—as something dedicated readers and writers do. When my students see me persevering, they see there is a real purpose to analysis and revision.

PART 3
LESSONS FOR REVISING FOR POWER, CRAFT, ANALYSIS, AND CRITIQUE

What You Will Find in This Section

Revision offers amazing opportunities for writers to make sure that their intentions for their writing match what is actually on the page. In this section, you will find several strategies that are highly focused on helping student writers attend to their intent. You will see a continued emphasis on structure, one of the cornerstones of nonfiction writing, and you will also see work around the placement of information and the physical space a piece takes up on the page.

You will once again see the relationship between writing skills and reading skills made tangible. With their own choices fresh in their minds, young writers will delve into their reading, knowing that there are intentional moves that all authors make when composing. They will study these intentions with a practiced eye, noticing moves such as word choice and cohesiveness, and they will begin to look for possible bias.

I deliberately didn't include a whole lot on text features, or multiple main ideas, and other common revision lessons. This is because there are several books and resources available that handle those topics well. Some of my favorites include *Units of Study for Teaching Writing* by Lucy Calkins (2013) and the Reading and Writing Project, *Strategies That Work* by Stephanie Harvey and Anne Goudvis (2017), and *Craft Lessons* by Ralph Fletcher and JoAnn Portalupi (2007), to name just a few.

When to Use These Lessons

These lessons can be used almost anywhere in your writing and reading instruction. As always, they can be taught sequentially as part of a complete unit. Alternatively, you might find yourself picking and choosing based on what students are doing and pulling small needs-based groups around your assessment. You might decide to teach the writing lessons in a nonfiction writing unit only to teach the reading lessons in a unit begun several weeks later, perhaps even in a social studies or science unit. No matter what you do, the most important thing is to ensure that the writing lessons come before the reading lessons they are linked with. This is the case throughout this book; however, it is more important in this chapter than any other.

Preparing to Use the Lessons

If you would like to prepare for the lessons in this section, I have a few suggestions:

- Study your students' writing and reading work. As mentioned previously, it can be tempting to teach all students all revision and analysis strategies. But it is more likely that some students don't need some strategies, and others are not quite ready for them. Set aside 30 to 45 minutes. During this time, look over your students' most recent writing samples. Also, use this time to review conversations that you have overheard or had with them about reading their books or writing about their books. It is time well spent. If only a small part of the class needs a lesson, you can teach it in a small-group setting while other students work independently.

- Freshen up the books, articles, and digital texts offered in your classroom. By this time in a unit, baskets can get a little disheveled, and digital files can be a little overlooked. You might decide to replace old standards with newer texts that you had packed away (or were just hiding in the back of the library). New texts for students to discover and devour can often get their blood flowing.

- Go hunting for student texts to admire. Katherine Bomer (*Hidden Gems 2010*) and Lisa Eickholdt (*Learning From Classmates 2015*) have written extensively about the power of using students' writing as mentors for their classmates. As students work hard on their revision, you might want to share particularly inspiring work and name the strategies those students have used so that other learners can follow suit.

writing

DECIDING WHAT'S MOST IMPORTANT TO REVISE

Lesson steps

1. Have students imagine a real-life situation where it's easy to get caught up in the little details and lose sight of the purpose.

2. Explain that this can happen to writers when they focus too much on strategy and not enough on their purpose.

3. Teach them to reflect about the reason for their writing by jotting it down.

4. Encourage them to place that note someplace where they will see it regularly.

5. Have them highlight parts of their draft that already address the most important aspects of their writing.

What I Say to Students

Imagine for a second that you just tried to throw a birthday party for a friend. You picked the decorations, you planned the food, you sent out the invitations, and you planned the games. You were so excited about all of the things you were doing for the party! But then, on the day of the party, you realized you forgot to tell the friend whose birthday it was! You completely forgot the whole reason you did all of that planning and setting up in the first place!

Sometimes, this can happen to us when we are writing and revising. We can get so caught up in all of the cool little tricks and strategies that we learn—ways to make the writing extra fancy—that we completely forget about the main event—the purpose for why we are writing in the first place. And we don't want to do that.

Before we launch into any special revision strategy we want to try, we should actually spend some time reflecting on what we really want to say in this piece of writing. What is most important for our readers to get? Then, we can jot those thoughts down or tell a friend.

PURPOSE

Students learn to reflect on the purpose of their piece and to consider areas that might need revision in order to align their writing with what they are really trying to say.

LESSON INTENDED FOR

- Personal expertise books
- Content-specific books or reports
- Oral reports
- Research reports
- Students in a wide range of levels

MATERIALS NEEDED

- Short analogy about losing sight of purpose
- Sticky notes or index cards
- Highlighters, colored pencils, or digital tools that allow students to highlight
- Student drafts and writing notebooks

I'm going to pass out some sticky notes. Please take a few minutes to reflect on their purpose and write it down.

[Check in with students as they work. If they would benefit from a model, project a student example, and say what it's about.]

Here's a sample reflection from a student in another class who was writing a piece about dirt bike racing:

> It's important for people to understand that dirt bike racing is not the same as other kinds of bike riding. I want them to see that it is a fun and kind of dangerous sport. But that it's really cool.

Next, let's look for places in our drafts that point to the most important things we're trying to say. These might be places we could add to or develop with different moves in order to make that important stuff really stand out. Highlight these places.

In the days to come, when you are deciding where to revise and where to try your latest strategies, you can go back to the places you highlighted and expand there.

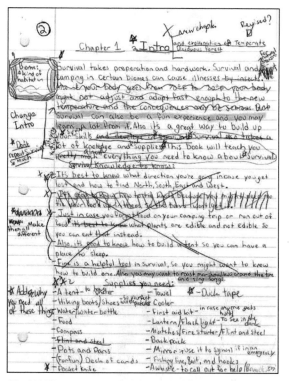

Olive highlights areas in her draft she wants to revise more.

Reading

IDENTIFYING AND QUESTIONING THE AUTHOR'S VALUES

Lesson steps

1. Make an explicit connection between the work they did as writers developing the most important parts of their writing and the work they will do to uncover what the author of the demonstration text values most.

2. Explain that they can read any nonfiction texts looking for similar moves in order to identify what the author most values.

3. Use a shared text to model, highlighting a few of those moves and noting what the author seems to give most weight to.

4. Ask students to decide whether they agree or disagree with the values they've identified in the demonstration text.

5. Remind them they can apply this strategy in their independent reading.

PURPOSE

Students learn to identify what matters most to the author and to question that value. They see the connections between what they found important in their own writing and what the authors they're reading seem to privilege, which helps them explore whether they agree or disagree with that value.

LESSON INTENDED FOR

- Reading high-interest nonfiction
- Trade books
- Articles
- Digital texts
- Textbooks

MATERIALS NEEDED

- A demonstration text that the students can use for practice, preferably one that can be marked up in a similar fashion to the earlier work in their writing drafts (I chose to use "Stars" from *National Geographic*)

What I Say to Students

When we spent time looking at our drafts and considering what was really important for us and then going back and highlighting places we could develop more to make those values pop, we were on the other side of the desk—the writer's side.

[Show a sample of a highlighted text or student work to help jog their memory about the work they did previously.]

Today, I want us to keep that revision work in mind as we read. Imagine us on the other side of the desk—the reader's side. Our role now as a reader is to recall that authors have intentions when they write—just as we did earlier when we revised—and that they often spend more time, space, and energy developing those parts that matter most. We have to look for those energized zones as we read, and we need to see them as clues to what the author wants to get across most of all.

What do those hot spots look and sound like? We may notice a greater use of adjectives or imagery. A passage may be beautifully written. Maybe there is a different cadence to the sentences, or there's a lot written, or there's a repeated pattern throughout the text. When we see those spots, we can underline or highlight them and then look back and analyze what the author did. From there, we can think about why the author did it. There are many reasons why—sometimes, the author does it to reveal awe, stir emotion, inspire action in the reader, convey anger, acknowledge his or her belief or skepticism . . . the list is long, but in one way or another, the author is convincing us of something.

I pulled up an article online about stars. I thought we could study it together, highlighting or underlining these spots.

[Hand out article, project it, or have students pull it up on their devices.]

Here's just the first part of the article. I'd like you to think about where you can see the author pointing to particular things that seem to really matter. For instance, there might be a lot of description, strong word choice, quotation marks, or other moves that shows us the author spent time developing this part because it matters.

> No one knows how many stars exist, but the number would be staggering. Our universe likely contains more than 100 billion galaxies, and each of those galaxies may have more than 100 billion stars.
>
> Yet on a clear, dark night Earth's sky reveals only about 3,000 stars to the naked eye. Humans of many cultures have charted the heavens by these stars.

Please take a few minutes to highlight places that stand out to you.

[Provide assistance if needed.]

Of course, just because we can start to identify what the author cares most about, that doesn't mean that we feel the same way, too. So our next step is to scan through those parts that really shine with what the author seems to really care about and then see if we agree or disagree with the author that these are really the most important parts. It doesn't mean we need to be vehement about it. Sometimes, we agree that what they think is most important is, in fact, important—but we might not agree that it is the *most* important thing. And that is okay. We are not arguing about whether or not the facts are true. We are arguing whether the facts the author is spending the most time on are the facts that we think are important.

With someone sitting near you or in your own mind, I want you to go to one of those highlighted sections and think, "Do I agree with what the author seems to think is important? Do I vehemently agree or disagree, or is it not that far off?"

[Listen to the students talk. Make sure they are not confusing disagreeing with the author's emphasis on one topic or another with saying the facts are not valid.]

Most of you are saying that you agree with the author that the sheer number of stars in the sky is very important. A few of you said you thought that the way humans use stars feels more important, and you would like to see more information about that. Either way, we can all see what the author thinks is most important by noticing how much space those facts take up in this or in any other text we read in the future. Then, we can use our own minds to see if we agree or disagree with the author's opinion.

Reading carefully to notice author choices

writing
REORDERING INFORMATION WITH INTENTION

PURPOSE

Students learn that the order and placement of information matters.

LESSON INTENDED FOR

- Personal expertise books
- Content-specific books or reports
- Oral reports

MATERIALS NEEDED

- A list of facts related to the same topic, each written on a separate large sticky note or sentence strip
- Blank sticky notes, index cards, or digital versions of these manipulatives for students
- Student drafts and writing notebooks

Lesson steps

1. Share an anecdote of a time when the order in which information was told made a big difference in how someone took that information.

2. Explain that it is the same for informational writing—the same information in a different order can make a huge difference.

3. Share information that could be included in the demonstration text.

4. Model a few different ways to arrange that information, making clear how the order of that information can have powerful effects.

What I Say to Students

When I was your age, I knew that if I did something wrong, the order in which I told my mom the information could have a big effect on how she reacted to that information. Let's say I told her, "Mom, I was running in the house and broke your favorite coffee mug. I feel terrible. I tried to fix it, but I couldn't."

I would be in big trouble. But, let's say I told her, "Mom, I have something to tell you. I feel terrible. I did something I knew I wasn't supposed to do. And even though I tried, I wasn't able to fix it. But I was running in the house, and I knocked into your coffee mug, and it broke."

I would still get in trouble—but not in nearly as much trouble as I would have been with the first version. That's because I started by telling her how I felt badly. I would have a little sympathy from her before I got into the bad stuff.

The same is true when we share the information in our informational books. We can place our information however it comes out, but then, we would be missing an opportunity to make our writing the best it could be. Today, I want you to walk away with this idea: placement matters!

Let me show you what I mean. I have a bunch of facts for my chapter on rats' relationships with people. Now, I already did a lot of work thinking about what's important in my topic—about what I want people to walk away from my book knowing—which is that while rats can be pretty awful, they have some good qualities too; in fact, they are complicated. So let's check out the list of facts that I was thinking of including in this chapter . . .

[Show a few sentence strips with separate facts written on each one.]

Rats can warn people of danger.

Rats eat people's food.

Rats can damage property: buildings, wiring, and dams.

Rats help humans make scientific discoveries.

Rats can be affectionate pets.

Rats can spread diseases.

Rats can be valued as part of people's spiritual beliefs.

Now, these are just a few notes. Obviously, I would write a bit more on each one. But if I were to look at each of these facts as information I would want to include in my chapter on rat relationships with humans, just the order would make a huge difference in how the reader would think about the information. Watch . . .

[Begin to sort the sentence strips into a new order.]

I could start with all the positive information about rats because I want to go through it quickly and then stretch out the negative information about rats, ending with the absolutely most horrific information.

> Rats can be affectionate pets.
>
> Rats help humans make scientific discoveries.
>
> Rats can warn people of danger.
>
> Rats can be valued as part of people's spiritual beliefs.

These are the positive facts—and now I can place the negative facts, organizing them from bad to worst . . .

> Rats eat people's food.
>
> Rats can damage property: buildings, wiring, and dams.

Rats can spread diseases.

Do you see how simply reordering those facts can change the way the reader takes in the information in the text?

I'd like you and your partner to jot on strips of paper some facts from the text you are working on—maybe five or six—to give this idea a try. Then, see how you can change the effect your information has on the reader by switching that order around.

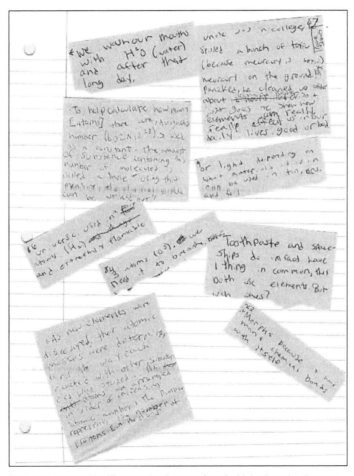

Doxie experiments with different orders for some facts for his book on the elements.

Reading

NOTICING THE EFFECT OF INFORMATION'S PLACEMENT

PURPOSE

Students learn to analyze how the placement of information influences the meaning readers draw from it.

LESSON INTENDED FOR

- Reading high-interest nonfiction
- Trade books
- Articles
- Textbooks

MATERIALS NEEDED

- A text for the students to practice with, such as an independent text or an accessible whole-class text (for this lesson, I use an excerpt from *Salt* by Mark Kurlansky)

Lesson steps

1. Remind students about the thinking they did as writers in terms of placing and ordering information in their writing.

2. Explain that they can use this knowledge to identify why an author of a text they are reading might organize the information in a particular way.

3. Share an excerpt of a class text and analyze together the order the author used when placing information in the piece.

4. Ask students to try this work in a small section of their independent book.

5. Encourage students to keep this in mind as they read going forward.

What I Say to Students

Just a little while ago, we were carefully placing our facts into our informational books. It was like we were experimenting with building different kinds of structures. Simply the order we used to lay down the blocks changed the way readers would look at the thing.

I know many of you started to think of your reading lives as well. You started to think, "You know, now that I'm spending this much time organizing information in a few different ways, I wonder if the authors of the books I'm reading do the same thing." And of course, you would be right to think that they do!

Today, I want you to look closely at a section of the book we're currently reading and see if you can tease out the chunks of facts. When you've blocked them out—you can jot them on sticky notes—you can then ask yourself, "Why do I think the author put the information in this order? What effect does it have on me as a reader that the information is in this order?"

[Project an excerpt of text for the whole class to study.]

HOW TO MAKE SALT

The four most common ways to find salt in nature are on the ground in dry salt beds, in the oceans, in underground springs, and in rocks under the earth.

Humans first found salt on the surface of the land, where ancient salt lakes had dried up. Animals, who need even more salt than people, were usually the first to discover these places, sometimes called salt licks because animals would go lick the salty ground. When humans wanted to gather this salt, they simply scraped it up from the ground.

The most plentiful source of salt is the ocean. But seawater must be boiled for many hours before the water has evaporated and only salt is left. This is a very expensive way to produce salt because a great deal of fuel, such as wood or coal, must be burned up. The fuel may be more valuable than the salt.

I notice that this passage starts with an introduction of sorts, which sets us up for the order we're probably going to find in this section. I also feel like he's placed the four most common ways to find salt in order from easiest to hardest. And if we just study the second paragraph, I notice that it starts by saying ancient humans found it—but then immediately goes into how animals found it first. Then, it goes back to the humans. I think that underlines the importance of how much humans relied on animals. If the author hadn't placed the mention of humans first, I might not have realized how important the animals finding the salt first was to humans.

Let's just try this with your own books for a second. Find a paragraph you read recently and reread it, this time looking closely at the order the author used for placing information. As you study that, consider why you think your author might have made that decision.

[Give students a chance to try this.]

When you go off to read today, this is an important thing to notice because it helps you to get another angle on an author's intentions. But it is also interesting to look at more than one book on the same topic and see the order different authors used for the same information. It really allows us to see all of the different intentions and uses for different information.

Analyzing the placement of information in different texts

writing

EXPLORING HOW WRITERS WEIGHT INFORMATION TO SIGNAL IMPORT

Lesson steps

1. Give an example of a situation where people wanted more of something because they particularly liked it.

2. Explain that writers do the same thing with their information: they include more information when they care more about a topic or subtopic.

3. Demonstrate revising a text to add more writing about sections that matter more, and think aloud deciding what to cut in order to accommodate the new elaborations.

4. Remind students that this is something they might want to try in their own revision work.

What I Say to Students

This past weekend I went to an ice cream shop with a bunch of people. We all decided to get sundaes. But what we got on the sundae was different, depending on what mattered most to us. I went with the classic—vanilla ice cream, hot fudge, whipped cream, nuts, and one cherry on top. My friend loves chocolate, so she had chocolate ice cream, hot fudge, and chocolate sprinkles, all on top of a brownie! I bet you can already imagine what my fruit-loving friend went with—can't you?

When we make choices in many different things in life, what matters to us shows in the things we do and the things we create. For instance, if we think soccer is very important, we spend time practicing it, watching it on television, and playing in games on weekends. If reading really matters to us, we have books everywhere, we spend time in libraries, and we read all

PURPOSE

Students learn the concept of weight in writing, which a writer attends to both intuitively and deliberately, giving adequate space to the most vital information.

LESSON INTENDED FOR

- Personal expertise books
- Content-specific books or reports
- Research projects
- Digital projects
- Oral reports

MATERIALS NEEDED

- A section of draft demonstration text where each part is almost equal in length
- Student drafts and writing notebooks

the time. As writers, when we are revising our drafts, we want to make sure that the parts that matter most to us about our topic and about our piece in general take up the most space on the page.

Let me go and look at my draft about rat bodies to see if I need to add more weight to my draft.

Now, before I even reread the draft, I want to be sure I am clear I know what I value most of all in my book in general and in this chapter in particular.

[Pause to show thinking.]

I would have to say still that my book is meant to show that rats are complex—they aren't all horrible or all incredible. And I think this chapter fits into that because I want to show that their bodies are rather amazing—but they are also kind of gross, too. Like, I really think that their fur and all that happens with their fur is one of the perfect examples of that. Let me look at this section on rat bodies and see how I did . . .

> Rats bodies are built to support their many amazing feats. They have noses with a huge sense of smell that allows them to smell not only from long distances but also a lot of scents that humans cannot smell. Rats also get a lot of information about the world through their noses. For example, they can recognize other rats from their own clans, see which rats are dominant, and, of course, find out when there is food.
>
> Rats also have incredible sharp teeth that can cut through hard surfaces like wood, cement, and even some metals. Another amazing feature of rats is the way their bodies are covered with fur. They use the oil from their fur to mark the trails they follow. Rat tails are not just used to communicate—although they can be used for that. But rat tails are also a way for rats to balance. Tails are also helpful for testing temperature and to hold on to things like wires and railings.

Now, I could hear some of you whispering when I was reading. I heard one of you say, "It's almost like she thinks the nose is the most important because it takes up so much more space on the page than anything else. She hardly has anything at all about the fur!" And you would be right. This discovery is so strange to me because I know so much about the fur, but somehow, it didn't end up in this section.

[Highlight or underline sections that need to be added to or trimmed.]

Now, I need to make some revision choices. Should I trim the stuff about the nose? I don't think so. I like it. But I do think I probably need to do some big stretching out of the sections on fur. For instance, I should mention how many colors it comes in, how it is very soft—so soft that some people have even used it to make fur coats and fooled people who wanted more luxurious furs.

Before you head off to write today, please take a few minutes to talk with a partner about what really matters to you. Then, look at one section to see if what you value most is taking up the most space on your page.

In Fiona's original draft of her chapter on fashion, skills only took up one page, even though it was the most important idea.

Fiona

Table ★ Of ★ Contents

1

In Fiona's last revisions, her chapter on fashion skills grew to three pages in length, showing the importance of that subtopic in her book.

Reading

LOOKING AT TEXTS TO SEE HOW VOLUME CAN SIGNIFY IMPORTANCE

Lesson steps

1. Make a connection to the work students did in writing earlier as a way to see what they can notice as readers.

2. Ask them to look at an excerpt of a text to see if they can identify what the author's purpose is, based on the decisions the author makes.

3. Have students share with partners what they notice in terms of weight.

4. Debrief by pointing out that knowing some of the moves writers make to take up space in a piece of writing can help students identify those moves as readers.

PURPOSE

Students continue to consider the connection between the author's purpose and how the author uses space.

LESSON INTENDED FOR

- Reading high-interest nonfiction
- Trade books
- Articles
- Textbooks
- Digital texts

MATERIALS NEEDED

- An informational text for the students to practice with, such as an independent text or an accessible whole-class text (for this lesson, I use *Disgusting History* by James A. Corrick and Christopher Forest)

What I Say to Students

Remember how earlier we worked as writers to make sure that what we thought mattered most to us as writers was represented by the amount of space it takes up on the page? I know many of you were already making the connection to how we could use that knowledge as writers to help us see what the authors of the texts that we're reading could be up to.

[Project excerpt of text to study.]

Let's see if we're right. Let's see if by simply looking at this paragraph we can see what matters most to the authors—at least in this section of text—simply by noticing what kind of weight the authors seem to be putting on that topic.

Let's look at this section about the Roman Empire from *Disgusting History*. As we read it, think about what is taking up the most weight and what that is telling you about what the authors value—or at least what they think is most important in this section.

The Romans grew rich off their empire. Gold, silver, and other treasures flowed into the city. There were large public buildings and many expensive homes. There was also a sports arena and two racetracks.

But Rome was not all gold and riches. Garbage filled the streets in the poorer parts of the city. There was also plenty of human and animal waste. Only the very rich had running water. Human waste piled up outside apartment buildings. Animals lived on the streets, dropping waste as they moved about.

[Give students time to talk in partners and then call them back together.]

I could tell that a lot of you were noticing that at first glance you thought this whole section was going to be about rich people. Then, it seemed like it was about poor people. But after looking at the actual sentences, it seemed like what the author really valued was showing the differences between the different levels of wealth and how different their lives were.

I can tell that some of you are already excited to use this same lens as you go into your reading. Keep asking yourself, "What is the author giving weight to?"

Discussing the author's purpose and use of space

writing

THE POWER OF STORY

Lesson steps

1. Tell students something about their school that is purely informational and expository.

2. Tell the same information but this time as part of an anecdote.

3. Have students compare the two examples and notice the different effects the examples had on them.

4. Point out that one revision strategy writers might try is to incorporate stories into their writing.

5. Introduce the chart, which explains the reasons that informational writers might incorporate stories.

6. Encourage students to consider adding this move to their arsenals.

What I Say to Students

Writers, I think many of you have noticed that our school has really increased the focus on helping our environment. There are several things our school is doing, but let's start with what is happening in the cafeteria. When students are finished with their meals, they do one of three things with their waste. They put it in the compost bin, the recycling bin, or the trash bin.

[Stop and let the students digest the information.]

Now, I'm going to share that information again, this time differently. Yesterday, I went to have lunch in the school cafeteria. I was so excited to be there to eat with my friends and the students. It was a great lunch— one of my favorites—pizza and a small green salad with an orange.

PURPOSE

Students learn that including stories within nonfiction pieces can help readers connect with information, concepts, and ideas.

LESSON INTENDED FOR

- Personal expertise books
- Content-specific books or reports
- Digital texts
- Research projects

MATERIALS NEEDED

- Two versions of a demonstration informational text: one with a story included and one without
- Student drafts
- "Some Reasons Informational Writers Include Stories in Their Pieces" chart (see page 108)

"This was so good that I ate almost everything," I told my friend Vikki. Then, I got up and made my way across the cafeteria to the garbage, holding my tray. I was a little bit nervous. I knew the rules had changed a lot lately. But I decided to just follow behind Vikki. I carried my tray to the station and saw that it was easy—there were three bins for me to sort my waste into: one for recycling, one for compost, and one for trash. The school has recently introduced a new system to encourage students to help the environment.

Writers, please tell your partner what you noticed about the first version and the second version of what I just told you. Discuss which one felt more effective to you.

[Circulate and listen in as students exchange ideas.]

A lot of you commented on how the story created a picture. You said that while you got the same information in both examples, the story helped you to connect right away. I heard some of you say that the story would help readers imagine the scene if they hadn't seen it before. Others remarked that the story details were a little entertaining.

Using stories in nonfiction texts is nothing new. I know a lot of you have told me over the past few weeks that you have seen stories crop up while you're reading nonfiction texts—some of them are more than just a paragraph or two. They can be pages and pages—sometimes even a whole chapter. And while it's true that not all information can be told using stories, a lot of informational writers do make their writing stronger and use stories to help readers better connect with the information. It is definitely one move you might consider making as you work on your revisions today. So let's just look at a quick list of why informational writers might use stories in their writing:

[Display this chart, which you can download from the companion website— and add to it with your students.]

Available for download at
**resources.corwin.com/
writersreadbetter**

Some Reasons Informational Writers Include Stories in Their Pieces

- To catch a reader's interest at the beginning of a piece

- To create a framing structure to contain the piece

- To make something difficult to understand easier

- To make a person or situation more sympathetic

- To allow the reader to connect to the information

- To elaborate on a piece of information

- To help the reader visualize

- To end a piece in a memorable way

Now, I am sure that there are other reasons that writers might want to use a story in their informational writing. However, just for us to do a quick imagining, let's look at this list. Then, I would like you to look at your current draft. Is there a reason on the chart that resonates with what you might want to do with your piece? If so, you might be the kind of writer who wants to try using a short anecdote inside of your nonfiction writing.

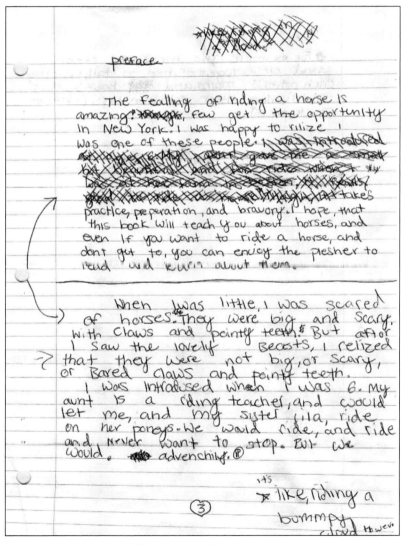

Maggie includes a story in her preface to draw in readers.

Reading

SWITCHING STRATEGIES WHEN AUTHORS USE STORY IN EXPOSITORY TEXT

PURPOSE

Students learn how to toggle between expository reading skills and narrative reading skills.

LESSON INTENDED FOR

- Reading high-interest nonfiction
- Trade books
- Articles
- Any texts that use a combination of expository and narrative structures
- Digital texts, including multimodal texts

MATERIALS NEEDED

- An independent text or an accessible whole-class text for the students to practice with that contains both expository and narrative elements (I use an excerpt from *Scrapes With Snakes* by Brady Barr)
- "Strategies We Might Use When Reading Narrative Texts" chart (see page 111)

Lesson steps

1. Tell a story about someone who is able to easily move from one skill to the next.

2. Explain that it is easy to use just one set of skills when reading, but it's important to be ready to use all of them.

3. Introduce the chart "Strategies We Might Use When Reading Narrative Texts."

4. Ask students to practice using narrative reading skills and switching over to informational reading skills.

What I Say to Students

My mother is a great cook. She can make anything. One thing I think of whenever she cooks is that she is the same person, but she can make so many different things. She just has different moves and uses different tools. So if she's making fajitas, she uses knives and a spatula and a skillet. But when she's making a cake, she uses a mixer and cake pans and a rubber spatula. Same person, different tools, different aims.

Now, why am I telling you a story about my mom's kitchen when I'm supposed to be teaching you about reading informational texts? It's because I was thinking a bit about our work in writing and how we were considering including stories in our informational texts for a variety of reasons. And I was thinking that now, as readers of informational texts, we'll be better prepared to know why an author might have decided to include one.

Of course, when you are reading informational texts, it can get easy to go on cruise control—just sort of keeping at the same speed, doing the same thing for miles and pages. However, not everything we read in an informational text is going to be expository—that is, it's not always going to be arranged around information in a sort of main idea and details fashion. Sometimes, the text will shift over to contain a brief story. In that case, we need to put down our informational tools and pick up our narrative ones.

[Display this chart, which you can download from the companion website.]

Strategies We Might Use When Reading Narrative Texts

- Pay attention to characters: their action, words, and feelings.

- Notice the events or plot of the story and how it affects the character.

- Envision the setting and connect it to the characters and plot.

- Infer what characters are thinking and feeling based on their words and actions.

- Interpret lessons, themes, and ideas based on patterns, symbols, and tone.

Available for download at
resources.corwin.com/ writersreadbetter

As strange as it may seem, we want to keep these strategies in mind when we are reading an informational text and then suddenly a story shows up. It's like my mom putting down her skillet and turning for her cake pan. Different cooking needs different tools. Different reading requires different skills. So let's try this right now—I'm going to have us read an excerpt of a text, and as we read, I want us to study what skills and strategies we are using as readers. I want us to notice when we are reading the expository parts and say to ourselves, "I need to do *this!*" and then when we hit a story, pause and change tools and say, "Now I need to do *this!*" Let's try it.

[Project or hand out copies of a text excerpt that includes expository elements.]

> Indian rock pythons can grow to more than 20 feet (6 m) long. They are incredibly strong. A python has more than 10,000 muscles (sounds like MUH-sels) in its body. Humans have fewer than 1,000. Pythons are constrictors (sounds like kin-STRICT-ers). That means they use their muscles to squeeze, or constrict, their prey.

Please chat with a friend and discuss what reading work you're doing here. What skills and strategies are you using?

[Give students about two minutes to talk.]

It seems like a lot of you were saying you were using informational reading skills, such as figuring out the main idea and noticing the facts and way those facts were organized.

[Share a section of the excerpt that includes narrative elements.]

> When a python sees an animal it wants to eat, it strikes out with lightning speed. It latches on to it with needle-sharp teeth. The teeth curve backward, toward the snake's throat. Once an animal is caught in those teeth, it cannot pull away. The snake instantly coils around it and squeezes. When the prey has died, the python opens its mouth wide and swallows it whole.

Please work with your friend again to discuss what reading work you're doing here. What skills and strategies are you using this time? You might want to look at the chart again to help you figure this out.

[Give students about two minutes to talk.]

A lot of you noticed that even though the character was a python, this was very much a small slice of narrative. I could totally see the little animal trying to pull away—just like I picture action scenes in my fiction stories.

I can infer that the python is very good at what it's doing—catching prey—because it does it fast and it doesn't seem to make any mistakes.

This is another story about the strong overpowering the weak. The python is the strong. The small animal is the weak. The python has more power and tools at its disposal, just like villains in stories.

You all know so much about reading and writing informational texts—as well as narrative texts. I just want to remind you that you carry those tools and strategies with you everywhere, so you should be prepared to be a different kind of reader at the drop of a hat, just like my mom can be a different kind of cook at a moment's notice.

Toggling between expository reading skills and narrative reading skills

writing

CONNECTIONS AND DISCONNECTIONS ACROSS PARAGRAPHS AND PAGES

Lesson steps

1. Discuss the importance of connecting different parts of a text in a way that is meaningful for readers and so the ideas link clearly across the piece.

2. Introduce a practice text that needs more connections.

3. Discuss strategies (chart) for connecting the various parts of a whole piece.

4. Demonstrate one of these strategies on the practice text.

5. Give students a chance to try another strategy on the same piece.

What I Say to Students

Recently, I was lucky enough to be in an airplane. As I looked out over the Earth below me, I could see mountains and forests and swimming pools and farms. I also saw something else: I saw train tracks and roads and highways and rivers connecting all of those things. I realized all at once while I was flying in that plane that without those connectors, there would be no way for people to get easily from one of those things to another. I mean, don't get me wrong—a person wanting to get from the office building to the mountain could just cut a path through the Earth. But there is no way that it would be easy for that person.

And of course this made me think about writing. I was looking at this really fabulous and fascinating piece of writing from a student from another class. And I really admired a lot of the moves the writer was making. There were surprising facts. Clear categories of information. The list goes on. But I feel like it might be missing the roads and railroad tracks that connect everything together. Let's take a look . . .

PURPOSE

Students learn that all parts of a writing piece should be connected in some way.

LESSON INTENDED FOR

- Personal expertise books
- Oral reports
- Content-specific books or reports
- Research projects

MATERIALS NEEDED

- A section of student-created or teacher-created demonstration text with few, if any, transitions
- "Nonfiction Writers Make Connections Between Sentences, Paragraphs, and Chapters" chart (see page 114)

[Project piece of writing that lacks connections.]

> *There are a lot of things to know about video games. People play a lot of different video games. There are a lot of different platforms and ways to play. These change all the time. Some games can be played on almost all systems and devices. Games like the Mario Bros. games can only be played on Nintendo systems. There are a lot of different kinds of games. Simulation games allow players to pretend to be in a world and sometimes even make that world.*

As writers, many of us use transition words and phrases. Words like *first, next, another example,* and so forth. And those words would certainly help this student. But it is also true that as writers, we want to make sure we are not just slapping those words on. Instead, we should be revising and writing each sentence, each paragraph, thinking about how the *ideas* connect to the ideas that come before and after it. Let's take a look at a few ways we might do this.

[Display this chart, which you can download from the companion website.]

Available for download at resources.corwin.com/ writersreadbetter

Nonfiction Writers Make Connections Between Sentences, Paragraphs, and Chapters

- Use words and phrases that were used in earlier sentences or sections to develop not only content but also ideas.

- Make reference to a term or topic used earlier.

- Ask questions that are later answered.

- Set up information in one sentence or section that is then fleshed out in the next part.

- Use a predictable structure (sequence, pros and cons, or cause and effect) that creates anticipation in the reader and cues the reader in terms of what to expect next.

Let me show you what I might try if I were this writer . . .

[Demonstrate connections using the student work sample. Mark up the text as you talk.]

There's a lot of good information here, and it starts out really clear and strong. And the writer does repeat a lot of the same words and phrases, which gives it some connectedness. I think one thing that would really help is if the writer also chose a structure of some sort, like maybe a question-and-answer structure or maybe a sequence. For instance, she could say at the beginning, "There are three very important things to know about video games." And then she could begin each of those three things with a numerical phrase like *the first, the second*, and so forth. So she might say, "The first important thing to know is . . ."

[Add phrases to the draft as needed.]

Talk with your partner. What else might you do to build that road from one section to the next in this piece? Can you identify a place that could be connected in a clearer way? How might you fix it?

[Give students a chance to try this work, coaching them as needed.]

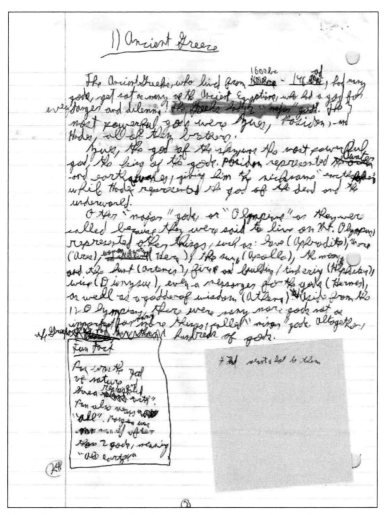

Isaac works on making connections from sentence to sentence and paragraph to paragraph as he writes about Ancient Greece, tying things together with content, order, and transitional phrases.

Reading

TRACING CONNECTIONS AND DISCONNECTIONS IN TRANSITIONS

PURPOSE

Students learn about how transitions and cohesiveness can help them to understand a text more thoroughly.

LESSON INTENDED FOR

- Reading high-interest nonfiction
- Trade books
- Articles
- Any texts that use a combination of expository and narrative structures

MATERIALS NEEDED

- A text to study that employs a variety of moves to connect sections (I use pages 8 and 9 from *Thunderstorms* by Chana Stiefel, which are side by side but visually quite different, which helps with this lesson)
- The chart on page 114 from Lesson 18: Writing ("Information Writers Make Connections Between Sentences, Paragraphs, and Chapters")

Lesson steps

1. Remind students that as writers, they are experts in making connections so they are equipped to notice cohesiveness in the texts they read.

2. Explain that sometimes an author makes connections that are less obvious; in these cases, students need to think about why an author would make those decisions.

3. Explain that places where there are connections and disconnections in a text are often places of deeper meaning.

4. Show how this works with a familiar informational text.

5. Encourage students to keep these tips in mind in their independent reading.

What I Say to Students

We've talked before about how every nonfiction text we read has parts. Sometimes, the authors have separated these parts with chapter breaks or headings. Other times, there isn't such a clear division. We've talked about how this influences us as both readers and writers.

[Point out the chart discussed earlier in the writing lesson, "Nonfiction Writers Make Connections Between Sentences, Paragraphs, and Chapters."]

What we're ready to discuss today is how when writers make the decision to connect different parts of a piece together, they are making one sort of statement. When they decide to disconnect the parts, perhaps by changing the subject or even the style of writing, like from narrative to expository, they are also giving readers a clear sign that these spots in a text are important.

[Read students an excerpt from a familiar text.]

THE MAKING OF A THUNDERSTORM

The warmth of the sun causes water to evaporate to form water vapor. Warm, damp air rises. As it does, water vapor cools and condenses to form clouds. If a lot of damp air rises rapidly, the cloud may form a flat-topped cumulonimbus cloud.

Cumulonimbus clouds are thunderstorm factories. Inside them, water droplets combine to form larger drops. Soon the drops become too heavy to float on the air. They fall as rain or hail.

MYTHS

Ancient cultures came up with their own expectations for the formation of lightning and thunder. The Vikings believed that lightning struck when Thor, the god of weather, threw down his great hammer. Thunder rumbled when his chariot collided with storm clouds. Early Greeks thought that Zeus, the king of gods, threw thunderbolts when he got angry.

If we look carefully at these two pages, we'll see places of connection and disconnection. This whole first page is stitched together in several different ways. There are connecting words like *as* and *soon* and repeated terms like *cloud*.

[Mark those words as you talk.]

And there is also a way in which this whole part is all about the same thing mentioned in the section title—the way thunderstorms are made. You might also be noticing that the author, Chana Stiefel, is making some of the same connection moves you made in your writing earlier.

But what makes this text particularly intriguing to me as a reader is that the author made a decision to disconnect one idea or topic from another too. We'll see that there's something important happening here. The first section is all about how thunderstorms are made. It talks about the scientific facts about the causes of thunderstorms, and it uses a lot of technical vocabulary. In the next section, on the next page, however, the author addresses something new. It is all about myths, the beliefs and stories people from a long time ago told to explain thunderstorms. One section: facts. Next section: myths. Both are related or connected because they are about the making of thunderstorms.

The disconnection is interesting to me. The author disconnects the sections by switching gears. In one section, all facts. In the next, all story. There is even a difference in the colors of the pages to help us see that there is a difference here. These don't go together. And that shows me, as a reader, that there is a deeper meaning here. For instance, maybe the author is trying to tell me that people have always tried to find explanations for things. Today, we use the scientific method, which uses facts. It would be easy to think less of people from a long time ago since we know so much more now. But the author places the myths right next to the facts and treats them with a respectful tone. I guess that one way to look at this seeming disconnect is that maybe it isn't really a disconnect. Maybe it's actually showing a connection—that myths were the science of the times for those people of long ago.

[Pause to indicate that you are done demonstrating.]

I know that some of you, while you were watching me puzzle this out a bit, might have formed different ideas for possible deeper meanings shown by these connections and this disconnection between these two sections. And that's fine. There's not one right answer here. Instead, I want you to see that, just like we made deliberate choices for when and how to make connections and disconnections in the pieces we are writing, the authors of the books we are reading make the same mindful choices. By noticing those bits, we help make our reading even stronger.

writing

VOCABULARY'S STARRING ROLE IN INFORMATIONAL TEXTS

Lesson steps

1. Share a story of a book, a television show, or another experience where the vocabulary used was very specific to the situation.

2. Explain that writers of nonfiction texts need to be sure to use the appropriate words for the topic they are writing about.

3. Ask students to create a word bank or list of words specific to their topics on a small sheet of paper.

4. Have students reread their drafts, looking for when they use those words and if any important words might be missing and need to be pumped up.

5. Ask students to revise orally, trying to ensure they are using as many of the words that are crucial to their topic as possible.

PURPOSE

Students learn that using the content-specific vocabulary is not only helpful for the reader but also helps make a piece cohesive.

LESSON INTENDED FOR

- Personal expertise books
- Oral reports
- Content-specific books or reports
- Research projects

MATERIALS NEEDED

- Student drafts
- Cards or half sheets of paper (one for each student)

What I Say to Students

I was recently reading the picture book *Dear Zoo*, which is a book for little kids by Rod Campbell, to my younger son. I've read it a thousand times, but that night, I noticed for the first time that there was a very specific type of vocabulary being used in the book: a lion was fierce, a giraffe was tall, and a frog was jumpy. And I realized that those words did a lot of work. Yes, they described the animals. But they were so specific that they allowed me to really understand what the author was describing. And because the language was consistently used across the book, I noticed that even when the pages seemed to go in a different direction, the words kept my son and me remembering that we were in a zoo.

This made me think about our informational writing and how we are all writing about very specific topics. Yet sometimes we are not using the specific language that goes with that topic. This is fine when we're drafting, but as we go back for revisions, it is important to make sure each word is exactly as it should be. This is especially true because all topics have a particular vocabulary. And those words don't have to be fancy. For example, if we were talking about school cafeterias, a few words I would expect to need to use when writing would be *trays, lines, cartons, sporks, tables, pizza,* and *students.*

One thing that can help us as writers is to spend some time thinking about the content vocabulary that we would use if we were talking about the subject, words that other people who know about the topic would expect to use. I would like you to take a minute and, on the card I have passed out to you, jot down as many content-specific words about your topic as you can think of. They can be nouns, verbs, or adjectives—whatever words you think are important to keep in mind when thinking, talking, and writing about your topic.

[Give students time to record their topic words on paper.]

Now, I would like you to take out your draft and lay it alongside your list. Reread your draft, this time with the lens of language. Every time you see a word that you put in your list, give yourself a mental high five. But if you notice a place where you could have used one of those words and you didn't, go ahead and add it now. I'm going to give you a minute or so to try it.

[As students write, rotate and observe, gently prompting as needed.]

Now, I want you to just look at the one part of your draft that you worked on—perhaps where you added a few words—and see if you notice anything about it. Does it flow together a bit better? Does it feel more like no one would mistake a sentence taken out of context as a sentence from another book? That's what we're going for. We want to be sure most of our sentences feel as if they could belong only to a book on this topic.

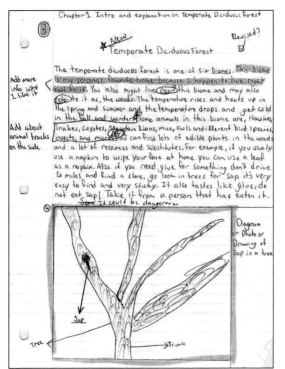

Olive uses content-specific vocabulary as she drafts and revises.

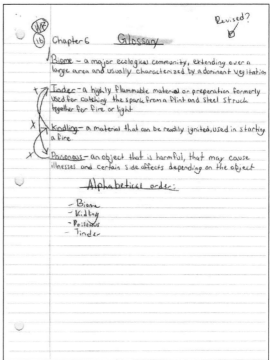

Olive also includes a glossary to help her readers with words she thinks might require extra support.

Reading

EXPECTING AND RESPONDING TO THE SUBJECT'S VOCABULARY

PURPOSE

Students learn that all texts have a certain vocabulary that matches the content and that when readers are prepared for that language, they will more likely be able to decipher it.

LESSON INTENDED FOR

- Reading high-interest nonfiction
- Trade books
- Articles
- Digital texts

MATERIALS NEEDED

- A text to study that has technical language, such as *Thunderstorms* by Chana Stiefel or another book used recently in your teaching
- Chart paper or another way to display student responses

Lesson steps

1. Tell students that vocabulary in reading is important.

2. Explain that when readers prepare to read a text by anticipating the sorts of words they might find, they are more likely to not only learn from the text but also to pay more attention when new words crop up.

3. Guide students to anticipate words they might find in a familiar text, charting what they suggest.

4. Have students read that text with those words in mind, noting where they anticipated correctly and making a note when new words are explored.

5. Encourage students to develop this habit whenever they read an informational text.

What I Say to Students

As readers, it is easy to just jump into reading a nonfiction text without taking a couple of moments to prepare to read it. The problem with doing that, though, is that when we come upon a word we might not know, we are more likely to either just gloss over it and read on without getting it, or we obsess on it and can't go forward.

I want to teach you a very simple trick to help this happen less. The strategy is almost the same thing we did when we were revising our writing for language. We pause, before we ever read a text, to think about the kinds of words we expect to find in this text.

Now to be clear, it's not a guessing game! I don't imagine that it is even possible to think of all of the possible words the author might have used.

Instead, we are getting our minds ready to notice unfamiliar words as we come across them, and we are getting our minds ready to do the work we need to do to understand them—at least enough to read on, searching for details that will help us define them further. Think of this strategy as another form of a reading warm-up.

Let's try it with this book, *Thunderstorms* by Chana Stiefel, which we were just looking at. If we look at the table of contents, we can pick a section that might be interesting to try this strategy with.

[Project the table of contents.]

Let's go with this chapter called "Weather Watchers." Since we know this chapter is inside a book about thunderstorms, we can make some really good predictions about the words we might see, as well as the kinds of words we expect to see. Let's chart some of the words or kinds of words you expect to see in this chapter . . .

[Quickly encourage the students to brainstorm possible words, and then, write them on the chart.]

storms

clouds

weather

people who watch weather (special name?)

equipment words

There will no doubt be words we haven't predicted. But there will also be words we have predicted. And also, there will be some very specific, technical words that we will learn. So let's try reading the first paragraph of this chapter. Let's see if any of the words we anticipated are there and also if we notice any new words that the author of this text might have been making a special effort to use. For a bit of a bonus, consider how thinking about the words before you read this section affected your thinking.

[Display the excerpt.]

WEATHER WATCHERS

A hundred years ago, people would look at the sky to find out whether a storm was on its way. Today, we tune in to current weather reports on television, the radio, or the Internet. Meteorologists gather weather data from more than 10,000 weather stations around the globe. Computers help them put it all together to make forecasts.

Interesting! In just this first paragraph, we got a couple of our predictions correct! The word *weather* showed up. And we learned a technical term for people who look at weather data: *meteorologists*. We knew we would see a word having to do with people because of the chapter title, but we weren't sure what word it would be. Predicting that we would see it made my mind ready to catch it when the author threw it.

While you're reading nonfiction, I want you to remember that we were prepared to meet certain vocabulary words as they came up. In fact, we were so prepared that the words we came across that we didn't know just jumped out at us, and we were in a better position to work on them.

writing

THE SLIPPERINESS OF FACTS

Lesson steps

1. Begin by displaying a partial, shocking fact.

2. Display the next part, which decreases the impact of the first fact.

3. Continue to dole out more facts, each one lessening the impact of the first.

4. Explain that informational writers can choose to include or not include facts that are helpful to the points they are trying to make.

5. Make clear that not all facts about a topic need to be included, especially if they have nothing to do with key ideas; however, sometimes leaving out facts can give a skewed version of a topic, and writers need to be cautious about that.

6. Have students try this with a class topic.

What I Say to Students

Let me share a fact with you about earthquakes.

[Display a partial fact, leaving a few parts covered.]

There were 3,836 earthquakes in 2012.

Talk to your partner about what you are thinking about that fact.

[Listen as students talk.]

Now, I know that is quite a shocking statistic. A very scary one, too. If I were writing a book about earthquakes and I wanted to scare you, I could just leave that fact there. But let me add a bit more . . .

PURPOSE

Students learn that it is not only the placement of facts that matter; what writers include, what they do not include, and how they set up facts within a piece also have powerful and ethical implications.

LESSON INTENDED FOR

- Personal expertise books
- Content-specific books or reports
- Research projects
- Digital projects

MATERIALS NEEDED

- A fact sheet on a class topic or demonstration topic, projected or copied for students (note: recycled facts from an earlier lesson work fine)
- A fact on a topic that has been written in segments or on cards (digital or analogue) that can be manipulated to be lengthened or shortened by covering or uncovering different parts

[Reveal an additional phrase.]

> There were 3,836 earthquakes in 2012. Of these, 2,297 earthquakes were under a 3.0 on the Richter scale.

Hmm . . . I can see some of you are thinking—hey, that's not so bad. More than half of the world's earthquakes a few years ago were so small that people probably did not even feel them. But I know a few of you are also thinking that there's still more than a thousand that we don't know about. That could be really bad. Now, as a writer, I could choose to leave you in suspense. If I wanted to inspire you to do your own research, I could leave it there. But my main goal is to prove that while earthquakes are scary, for the most part, dangerous ones are incredibly rare. So I can add one more fact to the list.

> There were 3,836 earthquakes in 2012. Of these, 2,297 earthquakes were under a 3.0 on the Richter scale. Only five of them were over a 6.0. And none were over a 7.0.

I know some of you are sort of surprised. I wasn't lying, but the way an author doles out the facts can have a direct impact on how the reader takes in the information.

Now, I can tell that a lot of you are dying to try this with your own texts. But before you do, let's try it with some facts we have used here before about rats. I'm going to give you a quick list of facts. Then, I want you and your partner to use this list to figure out what message you would want to send as writers.

[Display list of facts.]

- Rats' teeth can bite through concrete and steel.
- Rats' teeth will continue to grow—right through the bottom of their mouths—if they do not constantly gnaw to wear them down.
- Rats are excellent swimmers.
- Rats can jump very high—some have been known to jump as far as six feet.
- Rats have been observed tickling each other and giggling.
- Baby rats are called *rittens*.
- Rats cause millions of dollars of property damage and food loss every year.

[Give students time to discuss the list, and then, call them back together.]

Next, I want you to organize what you want to say, including some of the facts. Think about which ones you want to include. Then, consider how you might phrase something—being very careful to be factual—and try writing a few sentences down. Make sure that as you write, you keep in mind your goal for your piece: what do you want your readers to know about rats?

[After students write for a few minutes, gather them back together.]

Some of you were noticing that in this case, it was really easy to leave out certain facts. You knew that if you were trying to send a positive message, you would want to leave the negative facts out and vice versa. However, even though that's fine when those facts don't have anything to do with your point, if you are directly talking about a topic—such as rats being misunderstood—you would need to include the facts that might have led to that misunderstanding, such as the millions of dollars in damage that they do. You would need to include that fact so that you acknowledge the other side as well. Otherwise, you might ruin your credibility. In this case, you can pair the destructive fact—they cause millions of dollars in property damage—with the fact about their growing teeth as a way to make the point that they really are misunderstood. After all, rats aren't trying to destroy property; they just need to gnaw on things to keep their teeth from growing too long.

In other words, even though we can be crafty about how and what facts we include and how we include them, we owe it to our readers to make sure we aren't being dishonest.

Reading

READING WITH EYES WIDE OPEN FOR BIAS

PURPOSE

Students are reawakened to the idea that all texts have biases, even those that seem objective, and that authors may be unaware of the bias or use it deliberately to advance their point of view.

LESSON INTENDED FOR

- Reading high-interest nonfiction
- Trade books
- Articles
- Textbooks
- Online multimodal texts

MATERIALS NEEDED

- Two texts (projected or copied for students) that have clear biases, such as texts with opposing views or texts with the same side but different perspectives (I use excerpts from the Plymouth Plantation website and page 8 from *The Dreadful, Smelly Colonies: The Disgusting Details About Life in Colonial America* by Elizabeth Raum)

Lesson steps

1. Tell a story about a time when it was easy to overlook an author's bias in a nonfiction text.

2. Explain how sometimes this can happen when the reader has a bias, and sometimes it can happen because the author makes a move that creates the bias.

3. Discuss how readers can spot bias by paying attention to fact order, word choice, weight, and other craft moves the author employs.

What I Say to Students

I love roller coasters—absolutely love them. And recently, I was reading an article about how the Cyclone, one of the oldest roller coasters, was being prepped for opening day. And I was so excited about opening day that I didn't notice until a friend pointed out that the article wasn't really supposed to be about how great the Cyclone was. But rather, if I looked at the headline and photograph, I would see that it was supposed to be talking about how the Cyclone had stranded riders! And I had completely missed it!

But when I stopped to reread the article to see how I missed it, I realized that the reason I did miss it was that the author didn't put much weight on that detail. There was just one paragraph. The rest of the article was about the history of the Cyclone, how few accidents it has had, and how many riders there are in a year—mostly positive stuff. And I realized that I was letting my own bias get in the way of my clear vision.

Then, I thought, "I bet that's not the only way readers get fooled." I think a lot of us think that just because a text is informational, it must not be taking any sides. But that's not true. I know that as a writer, I am taking a side. I know that as a writer I have massaged facts to support my cause.

Today, I want all of us to learn and remember that all texts have a bias. Some have more of a bias than others, but part of our job as readers of informational texts is to make sure that we keep a critical eye out for those.

[Hand out copies of the two texts or project them.]

We're going to try this now. I have two short excerpts of texts, both on the same topic. We are going to read with a critical eye, knowing that all texts have bias, but our job as readers is to spot it by paying attention to weight, word choice, and fact order—all those things we did as writers to get our own messages out there.

[Display the first text, and read it aloud.]

> When the houses were finished, they were not very large. Because the Pilgrims hoped to own their own land and build better houses in the future, the houses in Plymouth Colony in the 1620s were not as comfortable as the ones the Pilgrims left behind in England and Holland. Most of their houses only had one room. The colonists did their cooking, eating, and sleeping, as well as other work, in this room. The women cooked around a hearth, where small fires were lit. The fire from the hearth provided heat during the winter months and light at night. Candles and oil lamps were sometimes lit too. If there was a chimney, it was built of timber and clay and clapboards just like the rest of the house.
>
> Most of the time, the houses were very dark. They had only a few small windows that closed with a wooden shutter. The floors were hard-packed earth. Some houses had a storage space above the first floor, called a loft. These spaces were used to store food and other goods, like dried herbs from the garden, bundles of corn from the fields, or even beds. They used ladders to climb up to the loft.

Please tell someone near you what this excerpt is about and what you currently think the author's perspective is on the houses that colonists, Pilgrims in particular, lived in.

[After a few minutes, display and read the second excerpt.]

> The first wooden houses were only about 20 feet (6 meters) wide by 20 feet (6 meters) long. Shutters over the windows kept out the wind, but they also kept out the light. A fire burned constantly to provide light and heat. Everyone ate, worked, and slept in just

one room. A lucky family might have a table and one or two chairs. Children stood while they ate their meals. They slept on the floor on mattresses stuffed with rags, cornhusks, or bits of leftover wool. Houses smelled of smoke, stew, and sweaty bodies.

Before we discuss the different perspectives, please say a bit to someone near you about what you notice this text excerpt seems to be about and what its perspective seems to be.

[Listen and give feedback as needed.]

I see that some of you can't help yourselves! I heard you saying that both excerpts were about housing in colonial times. The first excerpt was speaking specifically about Plymouth housing, but other than that, there were a lot of similarities. They both discussed the small size of the homes, how dark they were, and that there was very little furniture. However, the first seemed to be describing only the practical things about the homes, whereas the second one seemed to have a different perspective, even though it contained many of the same facts. The second one mentioned if a family was "lucky," they might have a chair or two, and it also mentioned "sweaty bodies." The houses felt a lot more difficult in the second excerpt because of the words the author chose to use, as well as the details to focus on. Mattresses were mentioned in both excerpts, but it was only in the second excerpt that we heard they slept on those mattresses on the floor, which was another specific detail that felt hard. In fact, almost every sentence seemed to have either a loaded word or a negative detail that made colonial homes not seem like great places to live—which shouldn't be a surprise, considering that the title is *The Dreadful, Smelly Colonies*!

I hope you are learning today that—just like you made craft, weight, and word choices to give a particular slant earlier when you were writing your informational texts—the informational texts you read have authors behind them who can and do make those same moves. In this case, the moves are more obvious in one text than another. But that's a good tip to know. If you suspect a text is biased or you just want to see which way it tends to lean, you can read another text on the same topic and compare the ways they handle the same information.

Students argue the facts.

writing

ADDING DIMENSIONS TO WRITING THROUGH MULTIMODAL FEATURES

PURPOSE

Students learn that digital writing does not need to be flat; instead, they can revise their pieces with an eye toward adding hyperlinks, videos, surveys, slide shows, and other digital writing options.

LESSON INTENDED FOR

- Personal expertise digital writing
- Content-specific digital writing

MATERIALS NEEDED

- A lift-the-flap book (in this lesson, I use *Little Explorers: My Amazing Body* by Ruth Martin)
- A typical book on the same subject as the lift-the-flap book (in this lesson, I use *The Ultimate Bodypedia* by Patricia Daniels and Christina Wilsdon)
- Two versions of a class demonstration text: one that has no multimodal features and one that has several

Lesson steps

1. Show students a lift-the-flap book alongside a book that doesn't have those features.

2. Discuss the ways digital writing can have layers like pop-up books do.

3. Share reasons a writer might revise to make a text multimodal (e.g., to convey information graphically, to make use of audio and video, to have more options for organizing a topic into subtopics, and so on).

4. Share a demonstration text that is digital but is flat, and compare it with the same demonstration text but with multimodal features.

5. Set students up to attend student-led or teacher-led seminars on various multimodal features.

6. Encourage students to reflect on the choices they make with their multimodal revision additions.

What I Say to Students

Most of you have probably seen lift-the-flap or pop-up books before.

[Hold up a copy of the first book, and place it on the document camera, lifting a few flaps and reading a page or two.]

This book is different than another style of book that is about the same topic.

[Replace the first book with a copy of the second book, and read aloud one page.]

What differences and similarities do you see between these two books? What difference do the features make? Please chat with someone who is sitting near you.

[Allow students to chat for about a minute. Jot down a few things you hear them say to one another.]

You were all noticing that a lot of the information was similar in both books, but one of the big differences was how they were laid out. For instance, in the lift-the-flap book, if we read a bit of information, and we notice that it happens to have a flap, then we can lift it and find more information, sometimes pictures, underneath that flap. It's like climbing inside the book a bit. And with the other book, some of that same exact information is there, but instead of being inside another compartment, it might be alongside another piece of similar information.

This variation between different styles of books got me thinking about different styles of digital texts. Sometimes, when we use a computer to write, we just type our words in and then print it out. While that looks very nice, it's simply a fancy version of when we use just pen and paper to handwrite our pieces. Those pieces are all flat. We can't dig into them. But as digital writers, we can also create multimodal pieces, meaning pieces that have a lot of different modalities or ways to get information across to our readers. We can use hyperlinks, video, slide shows, surveys, and graphics, to name a few.

Of course, writers don't just use those features because they can. They use them for lots of very good reasons. For instance, writers use the features as follows:

- To give background information by linking to another article
- To let readers see complementary information through several pictures in a slide show
- To let readers hear sound and watch movement about the topic through video clips
- To ask for information or opinions from readers in a survey
- To show a visual representation of information through a graphic

There are even more reasons than that, but let me show you what types of differences you might see in your own pieces if you decide you want to make your informational piece have some multimodal features. Let's look at the piece I've been working on.

[Display the first version of the demonstration text without multimodal features.]

RAT TAILS

Rats' bodies are amazing for a lot of reasons, but one of the body parts people probably don't think about is their tails. This might

- A few student-led or teacher-led seminar topics or groups with a sign-up sheet (e.g., adding hyperlinks, including video, including slide shows, creating surveys, and creating infographics or other features)
- A chart that describes reasons digital writers might include multimodal features (optional)

be because rat tails look a little bit like earthworms: they are long, pinkish, furless, and have rings around them.

A rat's tail is made up of bone, veins, and skin. The bone actually comes straight from the rat's backbone, so it is connected to the main part of a rat's body and is a very important body part. A rat's tail serves two main purposes: to help control its body temperature and to help it to balance.

While some animals might pant in order to cool down, rats use their tails to cool their bodies. When they get too hot, they send their extra heat out through their tails. When they get too cold, they keep their heat in their tails.

Rats also use their tails for balance. As you may know, rats can balance on wires and even the sides of walls. Part of the reason they are able to do this is because they use their tails for balance. A lot of people describe this as being similar to what a circus tightrope walker does. In a pinch, a rat can even use its tail to hold onto a tree branch.

Now, if I decided I wanted to give people a way to look more into one of my topics, I could add a hyperlink. If I wanted to give them a video with more information, I could include a link to a video site. If I wanted to get people's opinions on something, I could include a survey. You get the drift. Let's see what that might look like in my piece.

[Display the multimodal version of the same piece, and talk through the addition of a photograph and a couple of hyperlinks, clicking on features as needed.]

RAT TAILS

Rats' bodies are amazing for a lot of reasons, but one of the body parts people probably don't think about is their tails. This might be because rat tails look a little bit like <u>earthworms</u>: they are long, pinkish, furless, and have rings around them.

A rat's tail is made up of bone, tendons, veins, and skin. The bone actually comes straight from the rat's backbone so it is connected to the main part of a rat's body and is a very important body part. A rat's tail serves two main purposes: to help control its body temperature and to help it to balance.

While some animals might <u>pant</u> in order to cool down, rats use their tails to cool their bodies. When they get too hot, they send their extra heat out through their tails. When they get too cold, they keep their heat in their tails.

Rats also use their tails for balance. As you may know, rats can balance on wires and even the sides of walls. Part of the reason they are able to do this is because they use their tails for balance. A lot of people describe this as being similar to what a circus tightrope walker does. In a pinch a rat can even use its tail to hold onto a tree branch.

Now, I can see that some of you are interested in possibly including some additional digital features in your work in order to make your piece more engaging or to give your readers more information or to help them visualize or to get information from them. So today, we have an unusual setup. I'm going to ask you to spend the first bit of writing time today going to seminars taught by fellow students and by me. I have signup sheets up here. Each seminar is only ten minutes long and will be repeated twice. So you could go to two if you'd like. Or none. And if you go to a seminar, you can also teach other people back at your table what you learned.

This is a typical brown rat.

SOURCE: pixabay.com/en/brown-rat-animal-rodent-rat-nager-2115585, printed under CC0 1.0.

[After allowing time for two rounds of seminars or independent work, gather the students back together]

Now we have a lot of digital text feature experts in this class. If you need help with a particular feature you want to include, make sure to check the signup sheets and ask the students whose names are on the topic you'd like to learn more about.

As you work, I want you to resist the temptation to include something "just because" but rather to think about the effect your choices are having on the pieces you're writing and the readers you are writing for.

Revising a piece by adding multimodal features

Reading

MULTIMODAL READERS PRIORITIZE SYNTHESIS

Lesson steps

1. Explain that researchers say there is a pattern digital readers tend to follow when they automatically read, but this pattern is not good for comprehension.

2. Tell students that they can take three key steps in order to help them get the most they can out of their digital reading— preview, plan, and synthesize —and that synthesizing information is the most important step

3. With the students, coread an excerpt of a projected text, using the three steps.

4. Remind the students that they should try to do this same work whenever they are reading something digital that is important to understand.

What I Say to Students

I know we've talked before about ways that reading online is different than reading paper texts. We know that shiny screens can make our eyes tired faster. We know that it can be sometimes hard to keep track of where we found some sorts of information because there aren't pages to turn and every page starts to look the same. We know we have to be extra aware of whether or not the source we're reading is reliable or not. And there's one more thing I'd like to add to what we know about reading digitally. That is, a lot of online readers tend to read in what's called an F-pattern. They read the headline, the first or second features and paragraphs that are in the shape of that F, and then they skim alongside the far left of the article. This can give the reader a gist of what the article is about, but it doesn't really lead to strong reading. There are actually a few steps we can take in order to make our online reading even stronger.

PURPOSE

Students learn that in order to read digital texts as efficiently as possible, they need to make a reading plan that prioritizes synthesis.

LESSON INTENDED FOR

- Reading websites
- Reading blogs
- Reading other online content with multimodal features

MATERIALS NEEDED

- "Three Steps We Can Take to Make Ourselves Stronger Online Readers" chart (see page 138)
- An online article that can be used for whole-class practice (in this lesson, I use "Pavlof Volcano in Alaska still erupting, sending ash plume up to 37,000 feet")
- A place to record the class reading plan (optional)
- Student devices for reading time

[Display this chart, and read each point aloud.]

Three Steps We Can Take to Make Ourselves Stronger Online Readers:

1. Preview

2. Plan

3. Synthesize

We already know that the first step is superimportant for a reader to do. Whenever we preview a text, we increase our reading comprehension by a lot. So before we even read the text, we want to be sure we look it over, skim it, and get a sense of what it's going to be about. The second step—which can be a tricky one when we're reading a digital text because there are so many different ways we can read those texts—is to make a plan. We can ask ourselves, "How am I going to read this take? What will I read first? Next? Last?" And then the last step is to take all of the information we read and then to see how each piece fits together. This tends to be easier if we synthesize as we go, asking ourselves as we finish each part, "How does this fit?"

I thought that it made sense for us to try a bit of this together. I have an article that came out a little while ago. I thought we could try to do the three steps here and see how our comprehension is.

[Display the online article.]

Let's start with step one and preview this article. Let's look at the headline, notice the story highlights along the left-hand side, look at the pictures, check out any subheadings, and check out any social media shares. If you want to, this would actually be a good place to use that F-pattern; just know that all you're doing is previewing. Once you've previewed, talk over what you see with a partner. What do you think this article is going to be about?

[Give students a few minutes to preview and another few minutes to talk. Listen in.]

So most of you said something about how you expected this article to be about a volcano erupting in Alaska and that it is shooting up a lot of ash that is affecting airplane flights. You got all of this information from looking at the headlines, highlights, photos, and other text features.

Now, our brains are all ready to read from previewing. It's almost like we just made a container that we can now fill with all the information we're expecting. This isn't so very different from what we do when we read a paper text, but I think a lot of us, myself included, tend to forget to do this when we're reading online.

Moving on to step two, we need to make a plan for how we're going to read this text. What's going to go first? Are we going to watch the video first? Follow the hyperlinks? Decide as we go whether to follow the hyperlinks? Do we read all the text features first and then the text itself, or the other way around, or a combination of this approach? Talk it over with someone sitting next to you—in order for us to best understand this article, what should we do?

[Give students time to discuss a variety of options for plans. Take a vote to decide the plan's order, and then record it.]

Our Reading Plan

1. Watch the video.

2. Read the text.

3. Decide whether to follow the hyperlink if it seems important.

4. Read the social media features.

5. Study the slide show.

I know some people are sort of surprised that I am okay with you watching the video before you read the text. However, sometimes the video can give you some nice background knowledge and vocabulary that can help you understand the text better. And the reverse can be true too. So it doesn't matter which you do first; it's just important that you have a plan and that you try not to skip any of the most important parts of an article. So let's watch the video first.

[Pause to play video.]

You know, I think a lot of you are thinking that we should just follow our plan and go on to reading the text. But I want to remind you of step three, which is to synthesize. And we don't just wait until the end of the article to synthesize; we do it all along. So after we complete each chunk of text—in this case, by watching the video—we have to ask ourselves, "How does this fit?"

I want you to work with your partner for a few minutes. Instead of just discussing what the video was about, please discuss how this video fits into what we already previewed.

[Give students a few moments to discuss. Listen in.]

Now, let's read the first paragraph, and when we get to the hyperlink, we need to decide then if we're going to follow it wherever it leads us or if we're going to stick to what is in front of us now. Each time we read a little bit more, we will stop to ask ourselves, "How does this fit?"

[Lead the students through reading a few paragraphs and examining the social media posts, including the small details like the hashtags and captions.]

Readers, we could finish this article, but I don't think that's necessary right now. Some of you may decide to finish it on your own. Others of you are more interested in going off to read your own picks. No matter what you're going off to do today, I want you to remember that in order to get the most out of online reading, you would do well to preview, plan, and synthesize.

Making connections in multimodal reading

"I often find the entire writing process, both teaching it and living it, akin to preparing for a long trip. As I begin to prepare for a long trip, I go through the exploration phase, where anything is possible. Then, the process becomes more meticulous as I commit to choices, and I find that myriad details underlie each choice. All of this takes time. Then, there's the final phase, which for me is always a scramble. This phase involves more than incidental tasks like packing toothpaste or printing out boarding passes; it includes big things like making key decisions about places to visit, which can make or break a trip. Ideally, I'd like to make these decisions in a leisurely manner, but I tend to do them at the last minute either because I didn't know I should make them until this point or because I have only just found a vantage point.

The end of the writing process involves important decisions too. Initially, we might assume that the only thing we need to teach our writers at the end of our time with them is how to make cosmetic decisions, such as proofreading and selecting cover styles. However, it is much more likely that we will also need to teach them how to make significant choices about style, content, and meaning at this stage too. On our journey, we may not find out about the perfect little café or the secret swimming hole until we wait in the customs line. Similarly, many writers don't find the perfect magical move that will make their piece sing until they see the end of a piece in sight. The key, then, is to teach students that the decisions at this part of the writing process are both purposeful and urgent.

Through it all, the reading work keeps rolling along. Much of the work in the later stages of a reading unit on nonfiction texts will be about recycling old skills and testing them out with new challenges (reading across several texts, applying skills to different contexts, and creating a personal reading project). It is a chance for students to feel success in repeated practice, as well as to edge outside of their comfort zone. If, like many readers of this book, you are using the lessons in this chapter to supplement a preexisting reading unit or supporting reading skills within social studies or science, you might want to make ever more clear to your students that their work as writers will continue to feed their reading lives long after these writing pieces are through. As they work on their writing pieces and mindfully read informational texts during these final days, they can continue to practice all of their skills. If you are primarily using this book as a collection of trouble-shooting strategies to primarily support reading work, you will find some of the more sophisticated reading strategies, buoyed by teaching them in writing first, in this section.**

PART 4

What You Will Find in This Section

Writing. I will offer several strategies for helping students to polish their writing—for making sure that it is as polished and reflective of their intentions as they would hope it to be. This means there will be large-scale revision strategies, as well as strategies geared toward tiny editorial detail and publication decisions.

Reading. Hopefully, at this point, your students have read several texts. They likely have a strong depth of knowledge on one or more topics—whether these are class topics or ones of personal interest. They will be tempted to wind down as readers, even as they are getting psyched up as writers. You will need to maintain that sense of urgency in both disciplines, linking the writing work to the reading more tightly than ever before. One way to do this is to help readers to view themselves as scholars of their topics. Acquiring expertise in content is the main way that skilled readers can deeply analyze the texts they are reading. In this chapter, you will find several strategies that will help learners to continue to extend their reading skills while also consolidating their learning so they walk out of this unit with a clear set of reading skills they can take into future informational reading.

When to Use These Lessons

You might opt to teach each lesson in this section to your class, especially if you are using this volume alone to teach informational writing and reading. However, if you are using this text as an addendum, you will likely want to select lessons based on what final skills you want your students to have and be able to transfer to new situations. Some of the lessons in Part 4 focus on purpose and audience for writing and content and purpose for reading. You will want to bear those things in mind while making teaching decisions.

Preparing to Use These Lessons

As always, much of what you teach will come directly from what your students most need. I always suggest spending a half hour flipping through student drafts, looking for patterns and strengths that indicate what students already know, and what they are ready to learn next. You might want to study student jots or written discussions in blog posts or notebooks to get a sense of their thoughts on the texts they have been reading. If you are using this book as a full unit, this is your final chance to get students to where you want them to be as readers and writers of informational texts, so the time you put into collecting tools, texts, and creating charts that will best support and inspire your students will be time well spent.

For those of you with limited access to digital tools, this might be the phase you consider bringing them more into both the reading and writing process. Even if you do this only on a limited, only-a-few-students-at-a-time-have-access-to-computers basis, it is absolutely worth doing. Informational texts, in particular, are legion online. Students attempting to read online will find themselves faced with reading challenges that do not exist in their paper books. In this book, there are digital lessons in each part, which explicitly address and teach to these points. For instance, you may need to teach them how to sort out distracting advertisements or links for unrelated material. Also, a lot of online reading calls for students to contend with interactive features such as videos, slide shows, infographics, and adaptable maps and charts. Students likely need explicit instruction in analyzing those features, as well as synthesizing the information with the information gained from the main text. These points can be taught as they come up, or you might choose to try some of the specific digital lessons sprinkled throughout the book.

Additionally, many students are online makers of content and will likely produce (if they haven't already!) informational content for a wider, digital audience. Because of this, when preparing for this final phase, you will want to consider how you might optimize, increase, or offer digital access to all of your students. For those of you who have one-to-one digital tools, this might mean placing a renewed focus on how students are using those tools and making sure they are not simply doing the same moves they could do with an analogue text but with more bells and whistles. Instead, you will want to help students take advantage of as many planes as possible.

If you and your students can access a laptop cart or a computer lab, now is the time to make several reservations over the next few weeks and look into the best ways to digitally save student writing work and access school or district digital-reading resources. If, on the other hand, you have only a small handful of computers, perhaps a few desktops in the back of your room, this is the time to create a schedule that rotates small groups of students through them so that each student gets several opportunities to use them for both reading and writing. You might ask them to spend this time doing quick research, word processing, reading multimodal texts, or doing another type of digital work that feels like a capstone to this unit.

writing

FIRST AND LAST WORDS: INTROS AND CONCLUSIONS THAT ATTRACT AND LINGER

Lesson steps

1. Explain that you are excited to write an introduction to your informational book.

2. Demonstrate an introduction that is typical of your grade's first draft introductions.

3. Explain that introductions and conclusions written toward the end of the writing process can be better written to draw in and satisfy more readers.

4. Study a couple of video clips of various informational texts, focusing on the introductions and/or conclusions.

5. Have students help to revise the original introduction and conclusion, using the strategies observed in the digital clips.

What I Say to Students

I am ridiculously excited to be almost finished with my rat book. And as I was thinking about how I might write my introduction and conclusion to it, I thought, "Hmm . . . how can I make sure I write an introduction that entices my readers to read the whole book and then write a conclusion that leaves the reader feeling satisfied?" So I thought, "I know . . ."

[Write your introduction on a whiteboard or other display.]

Introduction:

Hi, my name is Colleen, and I am going to teach you about rats. Please read my book. Enjoy!

Conclusion:

I hope you learned a lot about rats. The end!

PURPOSE

Students learn that one of the most efficient ways to write well-crafted introductions and conclusions is to wait until they are almost done with their work.

LESSON INTENDED FOR

- Personal expertise books
- Content-specific books or reports
- Research projects
- Oral reports

MATERIALS NEEDED

- Your demonstration text with all the sections completed except for the beginning and ending OR a student sample with those two pieces not yet written
- A white board or other temporary writing surface
- Excerpts of just the beginnings and endings of nonfiction video texts, like the first minute or two of *Bill Nye the Science Guy* or the first two to three minutes of *Earth* by Disneynature (available for rental or purchase or from your local public library)

I can hear some of you giggling. Is it because you know that this is no way for writers who have worked so hard on their book to introduce or end it? I would have to say that I agree with you. Yet it is so tempting to do that, isn't it? We're so close to the end, and yet we still have a lot to do. Maybe people will skip those parts? But we know they don't. As readers in this class, we've talked so many times about choosing books and how one way we decide what to read is to try the first page or two. If we love it, we keep going. If we don't, we put it down.

Sometimes, when I'm thinking of beginnings and endings, I like to think of things other than paper or digital texts that use words. Sometimes, I like to watch television or films that are informational. For instance, I know some of you have heard of or watched *Bill Nye the Science Guy*. It was a very popular science show for kids a few years ago. Let's watch a little clip of it.

[Play a clip of the first one or two minutes of the opening sketch.]

Can you list what you just saw the people who made that show do in order to get their viewers ready to watch? Jot those down as a personal chart for you and your partner.

[Give students a few minutes to discuss and make notes. Listen in.]

I heard some of you say things like make jokes, tell a story, give a few facts, and mention what people don't know about the topic. These are all good ways to start.

Now, let's watch the first few minutes of the beginning and the ending of the documentary *Earth*. There's a totally different feel to this one. It wasn't just meant for kids but for all ages of people who want to learn about our planet. See what you notice that its makers do to introduce and conclude the piece.

[Show clips of the first and last two minutes.]

Now, just like before, I'd like you to record what you noticed the makers do.

[Give students a few minutes to discuss and make notes. Listen in.]

This time, I heard you talking about things like starting the piece by showing the sun rising and setting, showing the whole topic—the Earth, showing movement, and talking about facts about the topic. Then, for the ending, some of you noticed that they repeated similar images, there was more movement, they showed the sun rising and setting, and they offered fewer facts and more thoughts.

Now, we all have some ideas that we got from the video, and as you look at them, you might see ideas we could use in our writing. After all, most of us could be funny or share important facts or repeat images at the beginning and ending of our pieces. I'm going to ask for your help. Up here, I have my latest draft of my rats book. I would like you and your partner to try to help me write a proper introduction and conclusion using some of the strategies you saw in the documentary and jotted down in your notebook.

[Listen as students make suggestions.]

Okay, so some of you have suggested I tell a little story from the rat's point of view or an expert's point of view, like Bill Nye or the narrator in the Earth video. Others suggested that I sprinkle in facts through the story, such as descriptions and other information. A few of you suggested that, just like with the videos, I can connect the conclusion to the introduction. Let me try out some of those ideas in the introduction.

[Update your introduction to demonstrate some of the approaches.]

> Imagine you are walking down the street with your family at night. You hear a sound behind the trashcans that are just ahead of you. Suddenly, you see a large rat, perhaps 12 inches (30 centimeters) long. It has a long pinkish tail and grayish-brown fur. Your whole family is terrified. But you know better. You know you are looking at one of the most amazing and adaptable animals humans interact with on a regular basis: the rat.

Okay, and now I'll try some ideas for the conclusion.

[Update your conclusion to demonstrate some of the approaches.]

> The next time you are walking down a street and are lucky enough to spot a rat, you will know not only to keep your distance but also that there are quite a few things you can teach your companions about one of the most adaptable mammals that has ever lived.

Your ideas, the ones we got from watching the two video clips, really helped my introduction and conclusion get much stronger.

I am hoping that many of you consider returning to your own introductions and conclusions and consider ways to craft them so that they work in a way that matches the rest of what you are writing. You might even find it helpful to go back and find your own informational videos to watch for inspiration.

Ashley revises her lead to try to show Mozart's importance in her life and the world.

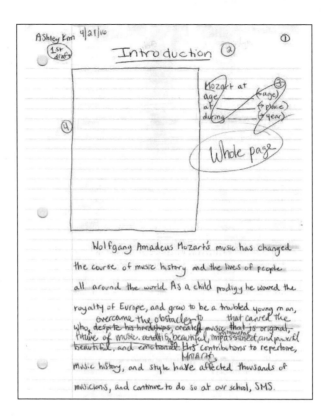

Ashley links her conclusion with her introduction to underline the important themes she developed about Mozart.

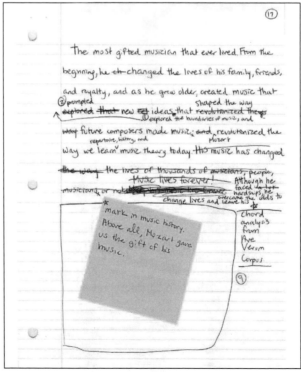

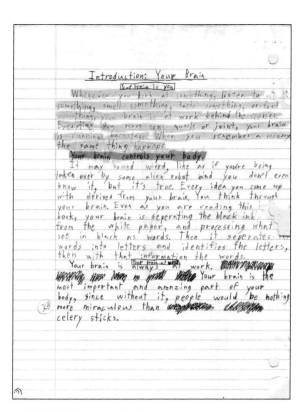

Sasha works to make a complicated topic, the brain, appealing and accessible to students in his first draft of his introduction.

Introduction: Your Brain

[Your brain is you]

Whenever you ~~look at something, listen to something, smell something, taste something, or feel something, your brain is at work behind the scenes. Everytime you move some muscle or joint, your brain is running backstage. When you remember a memory the same thing happens.~~

[Your brain controls your body.]

It may sound wierd, like as if you're being taken over by some alien robot and you don't even know it, but it's true. Every idea you come up with derives from your brain. You think through your brain. Even as you are reading this book, your brain is seperating the black ink from the white paper, and processing what see in black as words. Then it seperates the words into letters and identifies the letters, then with that information the words.

Your brain is always at work. ~~Your brain is~~ Your brain is the most important and amazing part of your body, since without it, people would be nothing more miraculous than ~~celery sticks.~~ celery sticks.

While revising his introduction, Sasha makes an attempt to elaborate, tighten some language, and show off a bit more in his writing know-how.

Introduction: Your Brain

[Your brain = you]

Whenever you see, hear, smell, feel, or taste something, your brain is at work behind the scenes. Everytime you move some muscle or joint, your brain is running backstage. When you remember a memory, same-same.

Your brain controls your body!

Sure, it may sound wierd; like as if you're being taken over by some alien robot and you don't even know it, but ~~it's true!~~ Also, ~~it doesn't~~ it doesn't work like that. Even as you are reading this book, your brain is deciphering the black marks on this page as letters, putting the letters more closely spaced together into words, and identifying the words and their definitions, and placing them together into sentences. I could keep going on with paragraphs and subheadings and pages and chapters, but it would start getting annoying.

Your brain at work

Your brain is always at work. Your brain is the most important and amazing part of your body; ~~and~~ without it people would be nothing more ~~miraculous~~ spectacular than cotton swabs. If you want to know more about this miraculous muscle, then you've come to the right place.

Reading

STUDYING AN AUTHOR'S FIRST AND LAST WORDS

PURPOSE

Students will reflect on the decisions they made as writers in order to help them identify similar moves in the books and other written texts they are reading.

LESSON INTENDED FOR

- Reading high-interest nonfiction
- Trade books
- Articles

MATERIALS NEEDED

- A copy of a text the students know well
- Books students have recently read

Lesson steps

1. Ask students to choose two texts they have recently read and bring them to the lesson.

2. Have them reread the introductions and conclusions.

3. Make the connection: Explain that the work they recently did to revise their leads is exactly the same sort of work the authors whose books they are reading do.

4. Explain that after reading a text, rereading the introduction and conclusion can give new insights into the author's intentions.

5. Discuss how beginnings of texts often foreshadow what readers will learn and conclusions often confirm that information and possibly raise questions for readers to explore after they close the book.

What I Say to Students

Readers, we're actually going to start this lesson before you even get here! Please grab a couple of nonfiction texts that you've read recently and enjoyed and bring them with you to the lesson. Once you get here, please reread the introductions and conclusions to get your mind ready. You can use sticky notes, highlighters, or other tools to help you keep track of those spots in your texts.

[Give students time to reread the material.]

Now that you all have reread some of the introductions and conclusions, I'd like you to think about why that might be powerful work to do on a regular basis as readers. To begin, think about the work you just did as a writer, crafting the perfect enticement for your piece and the perfect final facts, thoughts, or questions. Now, ask yourself, "What treasures might brave readers find if they decide to reread the introductions and conclusions of the books they are reading?" Take a few moments to discuss this with a partner.

[Give students a few minutes to discuss.]

Of course, there is no exactly perfect answer to the question because every reader and every writer is different. However, I have noticed that as a reader, when I finish a book and immediately go back to take in the beginning again, now that I have digested the whole body of the text, I often see things I did not see before—clues to main ideas, clear evidence of some authorial intent or bias, clues to what I will discover later, or a crash course in the whole text. I could tell a lot of you were surprised just now about how much you got out of the work when you reread the beginning and end.

Today, I want you to recognize that authors often use their beginnings to foreshadow what's most important in their text and endings to confirm it and possibly raise questions for readers to contemplate. We might not agree with what the author has left in our lap, just like the readers of the pieces we wrote may not like what we left for them. But it doesn't matter. Having that information makes us better positioned as learners to decide whether we agree, disagree, or are ambivalent about the text in front of us.

Checking a text for hints to information that will be learned

Writing

CHOOSING WHEN TO QUOTE, DESCRIBE, OR SUMMARIZE

PURPOSE

Students learn several ways authors can decide whether they should describe, summarize, or directly quote what they have learned from a direct resource.

LESSON INTENDED FOR

- Personal expertise books
- Content-specific books or reports
- Research projects
- Oral reports
- Digital projects

MATERIALS NEEDED

- Resource chart (see page 153)

Lesson steps

1. Explain that when it comes to incorporating information from sources, writers of informational texts have many choices they can make and reasons why they might make them.

2. Introduce the chart, which explains different reasons authors might make different choices when it comes to quoting, describing, or summarizing a source.

3. Encourage students to be mindful as they make those choices.

What I Say to Students

One of the tricky things for a lot of writers, myself included, is that when I am writing a nonfiction text, I sometimes just know the information because over the years, I have learned the information. However, there are lots of other times that I know I got the information from a specific place, or I just think it would be better for the reader to know the source the information is from, or I think quoting someone else would make me look more knowledgeable. But if I do decide I want to mention whom I got the information from, then I still don't necessarily know which way I should do it. Do I directly quote what the resource said or wrote? Do I just describe it fully in my own words? Or should I shrink it down to a summary? The categories on this chart help me figure it out.

[Display this resource chart, which you can download from the companion website.]

When referring to a resource, I should . . .

Quote if . . .	Describe if . . .	Summarize if . . .
• The resource said it better than I could • The resource said something particularly powerful, funny, or poignant • Most of the text is from my point of view because quoting allows the reader to get another perspective • I want to show a different point of view • I want to show a complementary point of view	• What the resource said is long and complicated and I shouldn't leave out any parts • I learned a lot from one resource and need to make sure to share most of it • The resource used was too complicated for my audience so it would be more accessible if I retold it	• What the resource said was long and complicated and I only want to use the gist of it • I want to lessen the weight or impact of the resource • If what the resource said was commonly known but I wanted to make sure it was included

Writers, as you look at this chart, I think most of you can think of places where you might want to do one of these three things for at least one passage when you are revising your work with the resources you have. When you make that decision, make it mindfully. Readers expect that authors make decisions like this for a reason.

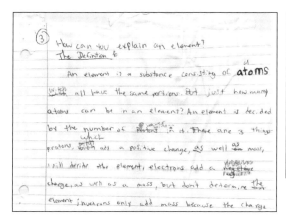

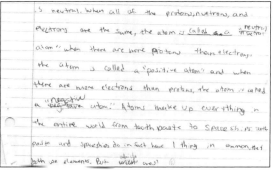

Doxie walks a fine balance between quoting, describing, and summarizing in his book about elements.

Reading

IDENTIFYING SOURCES AND CONSIDERING THEIR RELIABILITY

PURPOSE

Students learn a few ways to determine a source's reliability.

LESSON INTENDED FOR

- Reading high-interest nonfiction
- Trade books
- Articles
- Textbooks
- Online texts

MATERIALS NEEDED

- A list of excerpts with facts from different sources (the lesson uses facts about pit bulls, which you might choose to use). In this lesson I use the following:
  - An excerpt from *The New Yorker*
  - An excerpt from Cesar Milan's website, "Cesar's Way"
  - An excerpt from the American Kennel Club's website
- Access to an Internet search engine
- Student access to a laptop, desktop, or tablet with an Internet search engine, ideally one to one, although partnerships or groups will work
- "Four Checks to Help Determine Source Reliability" chart (see page 156)

Lesson steps

1. Explain that readers cannot take for granted that everything in writing is true.

2. Display a list of excerpts with facts about a familiar topic, including the sources, for students to consider.

3. Ask students to work with a friend to try to determine if the facts are reliable.

4. Display the chart, and review the strategies together.

5. Ask students to fact-check the material.

6. Encourage them to also check the facts for alignment across different sources.

What I Say to Students

I know most of you have read very widely on your topics. You've pored through some books, some articles, and sources on Internet sites. But as readers of information, we cannot take for granted that everything we read is true. No matter where you are getting your material—yes, this even applies to textbooks—we need to be critical readers, deciding whether or not the source (the text itself or the resource mentioned in the text) is reliable. So today, I thought we could take some time to talk about this.

When looking over information, I want to make sure I know where all of the information comes from. If I don't, that is my first warning light. I'm going to be very cautious in trusting that information, and I will want to make sure I get a second opinion on it. But if I can figure out the source, the next move I want to make is to determine if that source is reliable. Let's take a look at excerpts with some facts about a topic I know a lot of you have talked about: pit bulls. I want you to look at both the asserted facts themselves and the source they come from. Then, I want you to think about what your initial thoughts are about reliability.

[Display list of facts.]

> Pit bulls, descendants of the bulldogs used in the nineteenth century for bull baiting and dog fighting, have been bred for "gameness," and thus a lowered inhibition to aggression. —From Malcolm Gladwell, 2006, *New Yorker Magazine*

> Far from being considered a killing machine on legs, pit bulls seem to be an American favorite in the early half of the century—indeed, during World War I, the country itself is personified as a pit bull on army recruitment posters, and several pit bulls go on to become famous in the American military. Referring to an athlete as a pit bull is a very common sports metaphor through the 1930s, and it is meant as the highest compliment. There is also a famous racehorse in the late 1930s named Pit Bull, as well as a number of pit bull stars of early motion pictures. Frequently, pit bulls are associated with children, as in the *Our Gang* comedies, as well as with Buster Brown, both in short films and as the corporate mascot for a shoe company. The famous RCA Victor image of a dog and a gramophone also featured a pit bull terrier. —From "Cesar's Way," the website of Cesar Milan, the Dog Whisperer

> The AmStaff is a people-oriented dog that thrives when he is made part of the family and given a job to do. Regular exercise and training are necessary. They are natural clowns, so they tend to make training comical at times; they like to put a little twist on your training program. It's vital to keep it fun and interesting. A stubborn streak can make them difficult to train at times and will require patience and a firm, but kind, hand. —From the American Kennel Club

So readers, please read through these with a friend. Then think, "Hmmm, are the sources reliable? Are there any ways to make sure the information I am getting from these sources is reliable?"

[Give students a few moments to work with a partner. Listen in, and then, call the group back together.]

Some people might think there isn't a way to be 100 percent sure. And that can be true, but there are strategies readers can use that will help them be mostly sure that this is a reliable source. Let's take a look at these strategies.

online resources

Available for download at
resources.corwin.com/ writersreadbetter

[Display this chart, which you can download from the companion website.]

Four Checks to Help Determine Source Reliability

1. Check the author.

   - Who is the author? Does the author have any connections to the topic that might affect what he or she writes?
   - What is the author's purpose for writing this?
   - Does the author or source write for a respected or known site?

2. Check the date posted.

   - Can you tell when the piece was written?
   - Was it written recently?
   - Would the information be affected by the date? (History—maybe not. Science? Possibly.)

3. Check for quality.

   - Is the piece well written? Is it well organized, and does it use a rich vocabulary?
   - Is the piece very slanted to one side, almost like an opinion piece, or is it a more balanced presentation of facts?
   - Does the piece cite expert sources?

4. Check with other texts on the same topic from different sources.

   - When looking at other pieces written on the same topic, do you find an overlap in information?
   - Does this piece fit alongside other pieces that you see, or does the information seem very different? (That can be fine, but you will want to proceed with caution.)

Now, I'd like you to try a few of these things out. Go and look up the sources on the Internet. If you want, you could also look up some of the facts they mention and see if you can find those facts anywhere else—just to be doubly sure that they are reliable. You can use your devices or continue your conversation with a partner.

[Allow students time for fact-checking. Listen in to their conversations.]

Most of you seem to agree that these sources seem fairly reliable. Some of you pointed out that all three sources are known and have fairly recent information. The material also doesn't seem to be setting off any alarm bells of being overly biased or poorly written. However, a few of you noticed that there are other sources about pit bulls, not as well known, that disagree with these sources. When you come across disagreements like that, I would encourage you to look into it a bit further.

Readers, another strategy you can use when you see a few different sources at once is to look across the information to see what lines up—what do all of the different sources agree with? It might not help you establish which source is the most reliable, but it will likely help you narrow down the information to what is as close to factually accurate as possible. And when one or two seem to have very different information from the rest, then it is worth doing a bit more digging.

Checking sources to determine reliability

writing

CREATING TEXT FEATURES TO ENHANCE AND ADD INFORMATION

PURPOSE

Students learn that text features can serve different purposes, especially when they are added during revision.

LESSON INTENDED FOR

- Personal expertise books
- Content-specific books or reports
- Research projects
- Digital projects

MATERIALS NEEDED

- Demonstration text
- Short, informal chart on reasons authors might use text features
- Text features to use in the demonstration text, such as maps, diagrams, graphs, illustrations, and timelines

Lesson steps

1. Have students review text features they already know as readers of informational texts.

2. Explain, while referring to a chart, that while it is tempting to include text features for decoration, skilled writers use them for other purposes.

3. Demonstrate revising a model piece, carefully considering a few different text features.

What I Say to Students

Before we get started with today's lesson, please work with a partner to list all of the different text features you have run across as a reader of informational texts.

[Circulate as students talk.]

A lot of you said you've noticed labeled diagrams, photographs, fact boxes, diagrams, charts, sidebars, maps, and timelines. And there are probably even more. Those are just the paper texts. There are even more options if we are talking about digital texts. The thing is, it's tempting to go wild with text features, especially now that we're at this phase of the writing process. You may feel tempted to just slap them everywhere. Or, on the other end of the spectrum, some people just want to avoid them all together. However, I think most writers won't be tempted to fall in either extreme camp if they simply think for a bit about how, why, and when authors might want to include text features.

Sometimes, authors use text features to include extra information that didn't really fit in the body of the text. For instance, they might do some of these things:

- Include some fun facts or a little anecdote in a box along the side.

- Include texts features to give an example of information that is described in the main text. For instance, a photograph, diagram, or map might help readers to picture and understand what the author is writing about.

- Include information that is needed to understand the text but is not mentioned at all—or just very lightly—in the main text. Examples would be a family tree, timeline, or chart that makes the data easier to understand.

I have a few text features to show you that I have decided I want to include in my book—or at least I think I do. One is a labeled diagram of a rat's body. One is a timeline showing the history of rats. One is a fun-fact text box with strange facts about rats that don't go anywhere else.

[Display the text features.]

That's what I have so far. But I might find I need to create more, depending on what I discover in my text.

I'm going to go back to reread now, to consider if this section could use one of the text features I have already created or if I need to make something new or if it's fine the way it is.

Now, when you go off to write, some of you will be exactly ready to do some work on your text features. Others of you won't be getting to that for a little while more. Maybe you already worked on text features and want to go back and revisit them with what we learned today. I also know that a lot of you are just deep into your revisions now and aren't sure what work you should be prioritizing for today. Please make a brief personal work agenda for yourself today, including what you will work on first. Note what you will do if you have more time. Once you have your agenda set up, you can head to work.

Neurons and Nerves

NEURONS

Everytime you see, feel, taste, hear, or smell something, cells all over your body react by sending chemical signals* to your brain. These cells are called **neurons**. Neurons come in bundles. These bundles of neurons are called **nerves**.

NERVE PARTS

Nerves have different parts: the **axon**, the **dendrites**, and the **nucleus**. The axon is very long. The axon sends the chemical messages made by the neurons out into the rest of the body. The dendrites* recieve messages sent out from the axon of another nerve or the brain itself. The nucleus of a nerve is what keeps the cell alive. All cells in the human body have a nucleus that provide the necessary nutrients for it's cell to survive.

SYNAPSES

Nerves always move throught your body, catching signals and sending them along **synapses**. Nerves move along their axons. When nerves send nerve impulses out, the nerve impulse travels across gaps in the axons of nerves called synapses. A nerve impulse can only travel in one direction across a synapse. A synapse is like a one-way

Diagram of nerves including dendrites, axons, and synapses

Dendrites   Nerve   Nerve   Dendrites
Axon →   Synapse   ← Axon

*are like the hands of the nerves. They are called **nerve impulses**

*a nerve. They, which are about 16,000 dendrites stick out of

road for nerve impulses. CRANIAL NERVES

Finally, ~~nerves~~ nerves pass on ~~the an~~ an impulse to a special type of nerve, which there are only 12 pairs of in the body, that ~~sends~~ sends and recieves signals directly to and from the brain, as well as to and from other nerves. These nerves ~~are~~ called **cranial nerves**.

Neurons ~~SENSATIONS~~ create nerve impulses based on what your ~~senses~~ senses sense. All senses have **main sensations**. These main sensations are the only ~~few~~ things you can really sense. Anything else you sense than the main sensations are combinations of 2 or more of them. For the sense of taste, these are sweet~~sour~~, sour, bitter, and salty. For the sense of touch, these are contact, heat, cold, and pain. SPINAL CORD

All nerves move through your **spinal cord**. Your spinal cord branches out into all the parts of your body, so you can sense things everywhere around you, not just on your back.

Nerve Types Chart	
Name	Specialty
Cranial Nerves	These 12 pairs send and recieve nerve impulses directly to and from the brain
Sciatic Nerve	This is the longest and widest nerve in your body.
Sensory Nerves	These nerves take information from the senses and pass it on throughout the body.
Motor Nerves	These nerves send messages

back and forth between the brain and muscles

Vagus Nerve Controls simple body functions such as heartbeat and breathing

④

Sasha includes diagrams and charts in his draft for his book about the brain.

Reading

INTEGRATING TEXT FEATURES WITHIN AND ACROSS TEXTS

PURPOSE

Students notice how authors employ text features and engage in reading inquiry work in the company of other readers.

LESSON INTENDED FOR

- Reading high-interest nonfiction
- Trade books
- Articles
- Digital resources

MATERIALS NEEDED

- Four or five baskets with copies of texts that employ a variety of text features, such as photocopied excerpts of familiar texts, bookmarked online sites, or books with specific pages marked (*Note:* Each basket or digital file should be organized to focus on one or two particular text features.)

Lesson steps

1. Make the connection: Remind students that they just finished creating text features for their pieces and that they have often encountered text features as readers.

2. Explain that today they will be looking explicitly at text features, aiming to determine why an author has used each feature and how it connects to the rest of the text.

3. Set students up to work in small groups to read the materials in the physical baskets or digital files.

4. Ask students to read with this question in mind and to jot down what they think: What are the ideas or concepts that unite that particular text?

5. Encourage students to build and record their theories and questions about text features.

6. If time permits, publicly record students' questions and findings, paying special attention to text features. If students do not make a direct connection between the choices the authors of their texts made and the choices they made as authors, then make those connections for them.

What I Say to Students

I know we all have text features on the mind now because you have been adding them to your pieces. And I can tell a lot of you are already thinking of some of the more interesting ones you saw in materials you read over the course of this entire unit and are dying to go back and explore some more. You are likely asking yourself the questions we information readers ask ourselves all the time: "How does this text feature support the rest of this text? What is it teaching me?"

I've set up baskets at each table. I'm going to ask you to start at your own table. You and your team are going to read and discuss the texts at your table. Some of them will be familiar texts; some will be new. As you read, I want you to pay special attention to the text features. Before you move out of one table and on to a new one, I want you to think about one text together and decide how the whole text is connected. What are the ideas or concepts that unite that particular text? Then, jot those down. If you have time to look at another text before it's time to switch, go for it.

[Have students switch centers every seven to ten minutes so they can see a variety of features and have opportunities to discuss what they see. Listen in and offer guidance, interrupting the work time to ask questions and provide tips as needed.]

Readers, there is a lot of great thinking and talking going on. Lots of teams are asking, "What are all these pieces together on this page trying to tell us?" These are big questions—and important questions—that you should keep asking. Or you might be asking yourself simpler questions: "What order do I read these things in? Do I read the text or the features first? Do I read from left to right or around in a circle?" And here's the thing—I don't actually have an answer for some of those questions. Different readers prefer to do different things. You should try several ways out to see what works best for you. What is important is that you are aware that there are different ways to approach a text and that you are reading all of the text—even the captions and headings. Every little word should somehow fit into the bigger meaning.

Studying text features can be surprising

Writing

CREATING STRONG TITLES AND SUBTITLES

PURPOSE

Students learn ways they can create strong titles for their own pieces by discussing a list of exemplary titles and subtitles.

LESSON INTENDED FOR

- Personal expertise books
- Content-specific books or reports
- Research projects
- Digital projects

MATERIALS NEEDED

- Copies of several texts on display with interesting titles
- "Ideas for Creating Great Titles for Informational Texts" chart (see page 165)

Lesson steps

1. Share the titles of several familiar books with high-interest or noteworthy titles.

2. Talk through what makes these titles successful.

3. Introduce the chart, which has tips for crafting great titles.

4. Prepare students for the day's revision work, encouraging them to place the task of coming up with possible titles on their "to-do" list.

What I Say to Students

Sometimes, I think we start liking a book or an article even before we read it, when we hear or see a title that interests us. Let me list a few that I know you have admired as readers all year.

- *Oh, Rats! The Incredible History of Rats and People*

- *No Monkeys, No Chocolate*

- *The Story of Salt: The Amazing Role of Salt in World History*

- *How to Swallow a Pig*

- *Balloons Over Broadway*

- *How They Choked*

- *Poop Happened: A History of the World From the Bottom Up*

- *An Egg Is Quiet*

- *Vulture View*

- *Bugged: How Insects Changed History*

These are all great titles for a variety of reasons. For instance, with *No Monkeys, No Chocolate*—it's a surprising idea. We don't think of monkeys and chocolate going together, so it makes me ask questions. With *How to Swallow a Pig*, I get very curious because I'm not sure exactly what that book is about, but since it seems to have a fact it's trying to teach us about, I want to read it. With *Vulture View*, I am grabbed by the alliteration, and also, I hadn't thought about vultures and their perspective before. All of these titles attract readers' attention. They give a hint into not just the topic but also the author's stance or ideas about the topic. Some are playful. Some are lyrical. Most match the tone of the book they go with.

You might be wondering how the authors came up with such great titles. Now, I can't speak for each author, but there are some tips I can share, some of which my own writing teachers gave me, to help you come up with a title that is worthy of your hard work.

[Display this chart, which you can download from the companion website.]

Ideas for Creating Great Titles for Informational Texts

- Lift a favorite line from your text.

- Try alliteration.

- Use two words: a specific noun and a strong verb.

- State the text's central idea.

- Offer a clue that will be revealed after reading the text.

- Use shocking or surprising words.

- Match the title to the tone of the text.

- Use a subtitle to explain more catchy but possibly confusing main titles.

Available for download at
**resources.corwin.com/
writersreadbetter**

Today, I know you have a lot to do. Many of you are deep in revision work. A lot of you are working on text feature design and placement. But sometime—if not today, then within the next few days—you'll want to try out several possible titles for your text. Just pull out your notebook and make a list of them, using the tips from this chart and some of your favorite titles as mentors.

Lucy tries her hand at creating a curiosity-building title.

Reading

TITLES AND SUBTITLES THAT CONVEY MEANING

Lesson steps

1. Ask students to share the titles they developed for their informational writing and the reasons why they created them.

2. Explain that authors of the texts we read take similar care.

3. Use an example of a familiar text where readers can gain more from the piece by paying attention to the title.

4. Suggest that they should always read titles of the texts they are about to read, but they can also reread titles of finished texts to warm up their brains and revise their thinking about those texts.

What I Say to Students

Before we switch completely over to reading other people's texts, please take a minute to share with your partner what you ended up naming your book, if you did come up with a title, and talk about why you called it that.

[Give students time to talk a bit. Record some of their comments in a visible area.]

I love how many of you chose titles with such intent. There was a real purpose behind why you picked a particular title. For instance, a lot of you were thinking about how a title could help people remember what's most important about your book. A few of you said you love the idea of raising the reader's curiosity.

So it should not surprise you to discover that titles are not chosen at random—there is a reason behind every one. Titles are usually the first clues not only to the topic but also to the writer's central ideas and intentions. When we skip the title or just whiz past it without stopping to think about it, we are missing a piece of the text.

PURPOSE

Students are reminded how much heavy lifting titles do to engage a reader and declare meaning.

LESSON INTENDED FOR

- Reading high-interest nonfiction
- Trade books
- Articles

MATERIALS NEEDED

- The same texts with strong titles that you used in the writing lesson
- Chart from the writing lesson, "Ideas for Creating Great Titles for Informational Texts" (see page 165)

You might want to consider reading all titles carefully—and any subheadings, too—before you begin reading a book. But then, about halfway through the text and again at the end of the text, go back and reread the main title to see if it makes more sense now. For example, when we read *No Monkeys, No Chocolate*, we were all thrilled to get to the end and find out what the title really meant. And it completely changed our theories about the book. Initially, we thought the book was all about chocolate, but now, I think most of us agree it's about how plants and humans and animals are reliant on each other. We got all of that by thinking about how the title fit with the contents of the book.

When you go off to read today, warm up by first revisiting some books you've read whose titles you didn't pay so much attention to the first time around. Then, when you pick up your planned reading for today, carry what you've learned about titles and their importance into your reading.

Students discuss the effectiveness of some of their favorite titles.

writing

THE MANY PURPOSES OF PARAGRAPHS

Lesson steps

1. Ask students to jot on a sticky note their thoughts about what they believe is true about writing paragraphs.

2. Read their observations and explain that while much of what they know can be true, there may also be other ways in which paragraphs can be formed.

3. Send students on a short inquiry into what they notice about the paragraphs they see in the texts they read.

4. Ask students to record their new observations on a class chart or board.

5. Reflect on the fact that paragraphs can be formed in lots of different ways and are most commonly used as punctuation.

What I Say to Students

As you join me today, I'd like you to take a sticky note and jot one thing you believe to be true about how writers are supposed to make or use paragraphs. When you are done, please post your note on this wall.

[Allow students time to jot their ideas on sticky notes and post them.]

Based on what I'm seeing, I think I can say a lot of you are under the impression that paragraphs *must* follow these rules.

Things we have thought are paragraph "rules":

1. Have a topic sentence

2. Be indented

3. Contain three to five sentences

4. Be used at the start of any new idea or topic

PURPOSE

Students learn that real authors break all sorts of rules about "traditional" paragraphs and that, as writers, they can also explore these options during revision.

LESSON INTENDED FOR

- Personal expertise books
- Content-specific books or reports
- Research projects
- Digital projects

MATERIALS NEEDED

- Sticky notes
- A blank space on a wall or chart for students to place their sticky notes
- Several baskets of books and articles distributed around the meeting area (*Note:* This lesson can be done with digital files as well.)

Those all could be elements that paragraphs have or do, but paragraphs can also be different. Let's try to find some more elements to add to our chart. There are baskets of books all over the meeting area. Please grab a book and look for paragraphs. See what you notice about how the author seems to be using them. What do you find that is exactly what you expected? What do you find that is surprising?

[Allow time for students to study the books. Encourage them to share ideas as they look. Circulate and distribute new sticky notes.]

I can tell by the way the sound in this room is rising that there are a lot of new things that you just found out. Please jot down one more idea you developed. This time, I'd like you to start your statement with one of these sentence stems.

- I noticed that some paragraphs . . .

- Sometimes, writers use paragraphs . . .

It's important that we try to avoid words like *all*, *always*, or *never* because those descriptions don't really exist for paragraphs. Please post your sticky note on the wall when you're through.

[As students post their new observations, read them over, and look for patterns to share with the group.]

A lot of you said that paragraphs seem to be groups of sentences, most of the time. But there are such things as one-sentence paragraphs! You also said it seemed like paragraphs group things together, but there are many different ways the author might want to group things. You also noted that paragraphs make it easier to read a page, so that could be one reason to break information into paragraphs. Someone else mentioned that paragraphs feel like extra-long periods—like a form of punctuation.

When you are revising—and for those of you who are already editing today—I want you to remember what we've learned about the paragraph and to avoid falling into the trap of believing that all paragraphs have to be written one way.

Reading

SEEING PARAGRAPHS AS AN AUTHOR'S ORGANIZATIONAL TOOL

Lesson steps

1. Tell a story about something that is grouped or sorted.

2. Explain that noticing how information is grouped and the length of each paragraph can help readers determine what a text is about.

3. Suggest that each individual paragraph is important but so is how the paragraphs fit together.

4. Lead a whole-class reading of a few paragraphs of a familiar text while asking students to notice both individual paragraphs and a group of paragraphs and their meaning.

What I Say to Students

The other day I was in my neighborhood grocery store, and I was walking down the aisles, noticing how things were organized. One aisle of the store had all of the fruits. Each bin had a different fruit, and similar fruits were placed in side-by-side bins. For instance, all of the oranges, limes, lemons, and grapefruit were in one area, and all of the various types of apples were in a different area. I started thinking about how when we read anything, there are ways that material is organized. Authors who organize material tend to put like material together. Sometimes, it's a whole huge section, and other times, it's a teeny-tiny one.

When we read informational texts, noticing how the information is organized can help us be efficient and get the most out of the experience. And if we want to learn more, we can really study how a whole bunch of paragraphs work together to see what the author is really discussing or emphasizing in this part.

PURPOSE

Students learn to lean on paragraphs in a text to help them synthesize information and ideas.

LESSON INTENDED FOR

- Reading high-interest nonfiction
- Trade books
- Articles
- Textbooks
- Digital texts

MATERIALS NEEDED

- Class read-aloud or other familiar text, projected or with multiple copies for the students to study (for this lesson, I used *The Story of Salt* by Mark Kurlansky)

I thought it might be interesting for us to revisit our book *The Story of Salt* to study a group of paragraphs and to think about their organization.

[Display the text.]

SALT PRESERVES

Once farmers formed communities, they began to trade and sell the things they produced. For many thousands of years, the most valued item of trade was food. But, without refrigeration, food spoiled. It was discovered that salt preserved food by killing bacteria and drawing off moisture. Milk and cream could be cured with salt to become cheese. Cabbage could become sauerkraut. Cucumbers could be made into pickles. Meat could become ham or bacon, and fish could become salt fish.

Though it is unknown exactly when this was first discovered, it is one of the most significant changes in history. It meant that for the first time people could journey far from home, eating preserved food. In fact, food preserved in salt could be taken hundreds or thousands of miles away to be traded or sold.

Hence, when people had a good supply of salt, they could also have a thriving international trade, which in turn led to great power. On every continent, in every century, the dominant people were the ones who controlled the salt trade. Today, the largest producer of salt is the United States.

Reading over this section, we see right away that it is divided into three paragraphs. They are all about salt being a preservative, but the information about that topic is spread out so that each paragraph serves as a container for different kinds of information. If we look at the first paragraph together, we notice that it starts by telling us something that doesn't really seem like it applies to the big topic of salt, but we soon see that salt allowed people to change what food was. Each of the sentences in the rest of the paragraph is just a different example of food changed by salt.

Now, I'd like you to talk with your partner about the next two paragraphs. What are they containers for? What information is tucked inside, and how does the author organize that information?

[Circulate and listen in as students talk. Then, bring the class back together.]

Most of you noticed that the second paragraph talks about how salt allows people to journey away from home and how it includes details to support that. The last paragraph is about how salt affected bigger trade and wealth, and it includes some details to support that.

A few of you said that at first glance, the last sentence in the third paragraph, the one about the United States, doesn't seem to fit that paragraph. But then, when you looked at it again, you realized it really does fit because the United States is the wealthiest nation in the world.

So it seems like these three paragraphs go together because each paragraph is the precursor for the one that comes after it. The style is like cause and effect. When we look at it that way, it's almost a little difficult to imagine any one of these paragraphs without the other ones. And also, taking the time to think about what information is in each paragraph and how each paragraph is related to each other can also help you to recall what it was you just read.

Synthesizing information and ideas

Lesson 26

Writing

PUNCTUATING WITH INTENTION

PURPOSE

Students learn that each punctuation mark a writer chooses affects the meaning of the text and the way a reader will understand that text.

LESSON INTENDED FOR

- Personal expertise books
- Content-specific books or reports
- Research projects

MATERIALS NEEDED

- Multiple copies of a demonstration sentence or group of sentences that can be punctuated several ways (*Note:* students can also download copies to use for practice from the companion website.)
- Students' drafts and editing tools

Lesson steps

1. Explain that punctuation marks are the gestures and facial expressions writers use to get their points across.

2. Remind them of punctuation they already know to use and why they use it.

3. Offer them a short excerpt from a demonstration piece, without punctuation, for them to punctuate.

4. Show them at least two different ways it could have been punctuated to very different effects.

5. Remind them that when they are revising, they should be paying microscopic attention to their punctuation.

What I Say to Students

Have you ever had a conversation with someone and tried not to fluctuate your voice or make facial expressions or use gestures? It's a little tricky, isn't it? Because those things—those smiles and nods and finger points—are all things that help us make sure our message is getting across to our listeners.

When we are writing, we can't lean over our readers all the time when they're reading and say, "No—that's not how I meant for you to read it!" And since we can't nod our head or frown or give a thumbs down, the only tool we have to do that work, besides the words themselves, is punctuation.

By this point, you know that we have all sorts of punctuation tools: periods, exclamation points, commas, semicolons, quotation marks, and ellipses. And you know that people tend to expect them to be used a certain way. But you might not have thought about how the way you choose to use them has a direct impact on how readers read your words and how they understand them.

Take a look at these sentences from my book on rats. I want you to try punctuating them a few different ways, each time seeing if you can change the meaning or interpretation. Please share your ideas with a friend when you're through.

Rats have been shown to be helpful to other rats. When an experiment was done where a rat could choose to either free a fellow rat from possibly drowning or have a piece of chocolate a majority of the rats chose to help the other rat to escape the pool!

[Allow time for students to record their decisions and share with a friend.]

Depending on if you love or hate rats or are somewhere in between, you might punctuate this differently. For example, it could look like this.

[Project punctuated sentences.]

Rats have been shown to be helpful to other rats? When an experiment was done where a rat could choose to either free a fellow rat from possibly drowning or have a piece of chocolate, a majority of the rats chose to help the other rat to escape the pool!

Or it could look like this.

Rats have been shown to be helpful to other rats! When an experiment was done, where a rat could choose to either free a fellow rat from possibly drowning or have a piece of chocolate . . . a majority of the rats chose to help the other rat to escape the pool!

What you are trying to say is of primary importance, so in your own piece, you will probably choose to use punctuation in a conventional way that won't interfere with your reader's ability to understand your meaning. However, you may also wish to experiment with different punctuation options to make sure you express your meaning in the most effective way.

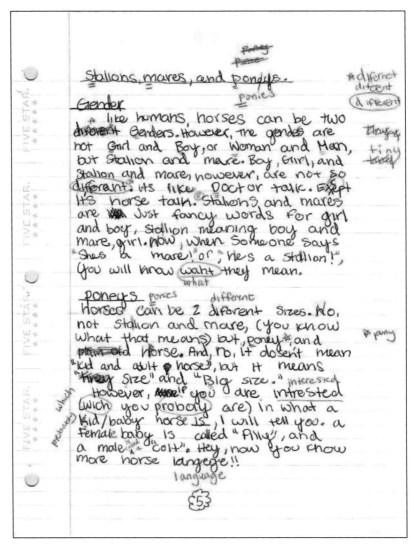

Stallions, mares, and ponyes.

*diferent
ditcent
a ireent

Gender

Like humans, horses can be two different Genders. However, the genders are not Girl and Boy, or Woman and Man, but Stallion and mare. Boy, Girl, and Stallion and mare, however, are not so diferant. Its like Doctor talk. Exept Its horse talk. Stallions and mares are just fancy words for girl and boy, Stallion meaning boy and Mare, girl. Now, When Someone says "Shes a mare!", or, "He's a Stallion!", You will know waht they mean.

ponies
Thayyy
tiny
teeny

Poneys ponies

different

Horses can be 2 diferent sizes. No, not Stallion and mare, (you know what that means) but, poney* and plain old horse. And, no, It dosen't mean "kid and adult horse", but It means "tiney size" and "Big size." interested However, more if you are intrested (wich you probly are) in what a kid/baby horse is, I will tell you. a female baby is called "filly", and a male. "colt". Hey, now you know more horse langege!!

*pony

which
probly

language

5

Maggie tries out a variety of punctuation while editing.

Reading

LOOKING ACROSS TEXTS WITH AN EYE TO PUNCTUATION

Lesson steps

1. Make the connection between punctuation and the way readers read a text.

2. Play a video or an audio clip of a newscast, and have students listen with an ear for punctuation.

3. Ask students to discuss what they heard.

4. Compare what they thought they heard with a printed transcript (optional).

5. Ask students to read two related excerpts, focusing on the punctuation in each one and noticing how the authors used similar and different forms of punctuation and the effect it had. If students have access to recording devices on laptops or phones, they can also do this exercise while recording so that both partners can hear themselves and compare with the transcript.

6. Explain that as readers, we need to attend to punctuation because it has a direct effect on pacing, meaning, and tone.

PURPOSE

In this lesson, students hone their eyes and ears for punctuation through close reading.

LESSON INTENDED FOR

- Reading high-interest nonfiction
- Trade books
- Articles
- Textbooks

MATERIALS NEEDED

- A video or audio clip of a newscast, with the transcript (if available)
- Two familiar informational texts on the same topic for students to read closely

What I Say to Students

Many of us spent a fair amount of time editing our writing to make sure our readers will hear our words the way our writing sounds like in our heads. Now, I want you to listen to a reader reading an informational text and see if you can hear the punctuation the writer originally used. Listen for periods, exclamation points, dashes, quotation marks . . . you name it—you should listen for it.

[Play news clip. Have students share the punctuation they heard the newscaster use.]

Now you can see how the punctuation really is important for readers—no matter if the readers are reading aloud or reading in their head. However, what you might not have considered is how a piece of punctuation can affect how you interpret a text.

If authors are using quotation marks, for example, we know that they are likely directly quoting a person or signaling to us that these words are not really their own words. If authors are using an exclamation point, we know they are referencing a strong emotion of some kind. And ellipses can mean so many things—that authors are unsure, that the idea is to be continued, or even that something in a quote has been left out.

Next, I'd like you to work with a partner. Please read an excerpt of one of the texts in front of you, focusing on the punctuation. Then, I'd like you to read an excerpt from the second text, also focusing on the punctuation. Keep these questions in mind.

- What are you noticing about the ways these authors are using punctuation?

- How is it affecting your interpretation of the texts?

- Are there any ways the authors are punctuating differently? Similarly?

[Allow students time to read and discuss the questions. Then, bring the class back together.]

One of the overarching things I hear you saying is that you hadn't realized there was much importance in paying attention to reading punctuation in informational texts. And now you're realizing that just one different end point or a dash instead of a comma can completely change the tone, meaning, and purpose of a piece.

Exploring how punctuation affects pacing, meaning, and tone

Writing

USING MEANING TO MAKE SMART SPELLING DECISIONS

Lesson steps

1. Explain that writers are sometimes judged on their spelling, even if that can seem arbitrary.

2. Discuss how making smart spelling decisions can help keep some of that criticism at bay.

3. Explain that knowing why a word is spelled the way it is spelled can help make us more likely to spell that word correctly the next time—and help us to spell other words like it.

4. Ask students to use resources to look up misspelled words in their drafts to discover why and how they are spelled.

PURPOSE

Students learn how to spell more strategically and conventionally more of the time.

LESSON INTENDED FOR

- Personal expertise books
- Content-specific books or reports
- Research projects

MATERIALS NEEDED

- Analogue or digital dictionaries and glossaries
- Lists of common cognates, derivatives, and root words
- Word-processing spell-checkers or other online spelling resources (if available)

What I Say to Students

One of my favorite linguists, Sandra Wilde, says that people only expect perfection in two things: brain surgery and spelling. Of course, this is ridiculous. While spelling is important, it's not nearly as important as brain surgery—or even the big ideas and concepts you are trying to get across in your writing. However—and this is a big however—a lot of people get really crazy about spelling. So one thing that we writers can do to protect ourselves is to make sure that we make smart spelling decisions. That way, even if we make a mistake, it's a smart mistake.

One way to do this is to understand which words you have trouble with and why you might have trouble with them. Sometimes, if you understand why they are spelled a certain way, you can think it through before you spell it again.

Here's an example. One day, I was working with a student who, when working with words that ended in the -er sound was never sure if it should be spelled like -ir or -ur or -er. And since there are words that all have those different ways to make those sounds, her confusion makes sense. However, when the student was trying to spell the word *cooper*, she wasn't sure which one to use for the end. So we went and looked it up online. We didn't look to find out how to spell *cooper*—although we could have done that—but to find out about that ending. Why does it end that way? We typed that into our Internet search engine. And we discovered that because most words that describe people doing things—*teacher*, *runner*, and *farmer*—have English roots, they all end in -*er*. So -*er* is usually used. Now, there are exceptions— like *doctor*—(which has Latin roots). But now this student knew that if she was ever in doubt on words like this, she could go with -*er* and would likely be correct.

My point is not for you to all spell *cooper* correctly! My point is that a lot of words have parts of other words in them. And if we can find out how and why words are spelled a certain way, then it helps us to know how to spell not only that one word but also a whole lot of other words that follow a similar pattern. Writers can do that by using a variety of tools. We can look in dictionaries to get the etymology, or background, of a word. We can look in word processors on our computers and actually read the explanation for why a word is spelled that way. We can also always look online. There are so many sites online connected to dictionaries or linguists, and these sites are filled with information on why words are spelled the way they are.

Today, I'd like you to go through your writing piece, looking for words you're not sure you spelled correctly. If you have a lot of words you are not sure of, you might just want to start with the words that are most important to your piece. For instance, if you're writing a book about sandwiches, you will want to be sure you spelled the word *sandwich* correctly.

When you find a word that is a possible suspect, don't just look up the word or ask a friend if it's spelled correctly. Instead, look up the part of the word you're not sure of. See if you can find out the history behind why it's spelled the way it is. Then, jot it down. See if you can think of any other words that fit that pattern—or, as a bonus, find other words with that pattern that are in your current writing. Start keeping track of those words as you work, and you'll soon have a small stack of patterns and words that you not only know how to spell but also know *why they are spelled that way!*

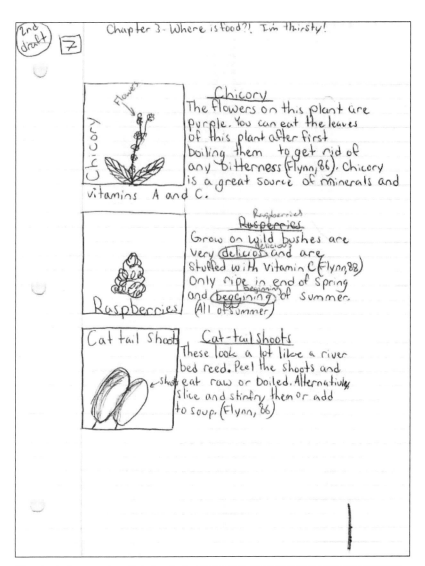

Chapter 3 - Where is food?! I'm thirsty!

Chicory
The flowers on this plant are purple. You can eat the leaves of this plant after first boiling them to get rid of any bitterness (Flynn, 86). Chicory is a great source of minerals and vitamins A and C.

Chicory (image label)

Raspberries
Grow on wild bushes are very delicios and are stuffed with vitamin C (Flynn, 88) Only ripe in end of Spring and beggining of summer. (All of Summer)

Raspberries (image label)

Cat-tail shoots
These look a lot like a river bed reed. Peel the shoots and eat raw or boiled. Alternatively slice and stirfry them or add to soup. (Flynn, 86)

Cat tail shoot (image label)

Olive checks the correct spelling of content words to avoid misspellings that could distract readers.

Reading

THE ROLE OF ETYMOLOGY FOR READERS

PURPOSE

Students learn that while context can be helpful for understanding what a word might mean, etymology can also be helpful.

LESSON INTENDED FOR

- Reading high-interest nonfiction
- Trade books
- Articles
- Textbooks

MATERIALS NEEDED

- A whiteboard or chart paper to record a word
- Analogue or digital dictionaries and glossaries
- Lists of common cognates, derivatives, and root words available
- Word-processing spell-checkers (if available)

Lesson steps

1. Remind students of strategies they already know to use when faced with unknown vocabulary.

2. Suggest a new strategy: looking for familiar words inside of unknown words.

3. Ask kids to try this strategy with an unfamiliar word that has a familiar root.

4. Encourage them to use tools such as dictionaries and online resources to explore more word parts that make up larger words.

What I Say to Students

When we're reading, we can do a lot of things to figure out what new words might mean. At this point in your reading, you are probably using the information you are getting from your growing expertise on different topics to help you. So you might find yourself just remembering a word from another book, or you might be relying on your content knowledge to give yourself a little clue. And context is definitely helpful. Also helpful is to use what you know about words in general. Look at the parts of words to figure out if you see any familiar other words within the word.

[Write an example word on the board.]

For example, if you see the word *bioform*, you might be able to figure out what it means because you know what the word *biology* means. Please take a minute to discuss with your partner what you think the word *bioform* could mean.

[Listen in as students theorize.]

What's great about reading is that the more you read, the more words you pick up. And the more words you pick up, the more words you are able to decipher by thinking back to other words that had similar parts. To help you in your work, you can use the exact same tools you used for your spelling work in writing, except that instead of using those tools to spell a word, you are using them to find out the history or roots of the word.

For instance, you might use the dictionaries or glossaries to look up the origin or history of a word. You could trace a finger down the cognates and roots word list to see if part of the word is there and, if so, what that part could mean. You could do a quick Internet search to ask for the history of the word or visit a popular dictionary website to get more information.

Some of you might be thinking that this sounds like a lot of work. After all, you could just spell-check it, right? But while that is true, it actually doesn't take very long to look up the history of a word. Maybe two or three minutes. And then, after that, just having that bit of knowledge in your head will help to make the spelling and meaning of the word stick, and you will be less likely to misspell it in the future.

Checking etymology references of unfamiliar words

writing

MAKING PUBLISHING DECISIONS BASED ON THE INTENDED AUDIENCE

PURPOSE

Students learn that an author's wished-for, main audience is a driving force in the author's decisions right up through the final stages of putting finishing touches on their pieces.

LESSON INTENDED FOR

- Personal expertise books
- Content-specific books or reports
- Research projects
- Digital projects

MATERIALS NEEDED

- A variety of professionally published texts ready to display or project (examples might include informational books, articles, textbooks, pamphlets, posters, websites, and nonfiction picture books)
- "Writers Consider Their Audience Before They Publish" chart (see page 185)
- Materials available for students to publish with, such as a variety of paper, pens, markers, fasteners, computers, tablets, and publishing software

Lesson steps

1. Share a few examples of familiar informational texts, and ask students to indicate whether they would be interested in reading them.

2. Point out that not everyone wanted to read all of the same things.

3. Ask students to explain what attracted them to one piece and not another.

4. Explain that writers need to keep audiences in mind as they publish.

5. Share the chart, which will help them consider their audience as they finish their books.

What I Say to Students

I want to share a few different informational texts with you. Some are familiar. Some are maybe new to you. I'm going to show you the cover or title and text features and read a bit of one. Then, I'm going to ask you to show me if this is something you would be interested in reading. Give me a thumbs up if you would definitely want to give it a read. Give me a thumbs middle if you think maybe you would want to read it. Give a thumbs down if you know you wouldn't want to read it.

[Display a few informational texts. Read a page from each, pausing each time to allow students to indicate their response.]

I noticed that not everyone gave a thumbs up to everything that I read. Please chat with a friend and discuss which texts you put a thumbs up for and why.

[Give students a few moments to discuss.]

What you are saying is so different! Sometimes, you and your friend totally disagreed. Other times you agreed. And that's because people have different things they like, different topics of interest, and different features that attract them. As writers, we need to keep in mind that not everyone out there is going to want to read our texts, but that's okay. Sometimes, we have a very particular audience in mind—like kids who live on the West Coast, or people who love animals, or people who prefer getting information from pictures rather than words, or mothers of twin boys who were born in February! (I'm kidding about that last one.) Other times, we want as many readers to like our writing as possible, so we are writing for as broad of an audience as possible. Depending on the audience you're going for, you'll want to make some final decisions in order to make sure you attract and hold on to that audience.

[Display this chart, which you can download from the companion website.]

Writers Consider Their Audiences as They Finish Their Pieces

Available for download at **resources.corwin.com/ writersreadbetter**

- Writers look to titles, graphics, and other eye-catching features to capture their intended audience's attention.

- Writers reread their tables of contents to make sure they've included all of the topics and information their audience might want. If it's not there, they add it.

- Writers reread their pieces, looking for things they might need to cut or revise in order to make sure it makes sense to their intended audience and will keep them interested.

- Writers revise their work one last time, making sure their word choice, craft moves, and facts match their intended audience.

- Writers make sure the form and format (book, article, website, or digital text) match what their audience most wants to read.

- Writers edit their pieces, checking for spelling, conventions, and grammar that might get in the way of their audience's understanding and enjoyment of their piece.

I want you to each look at this chart. You might have some other ideas in mind too. But in this, our last day working on our projects, I want you to be putting your audience first and foremost in your mind, just like you were at the beginning. And I want you to be sure that the people you are imagining would give you a thumbs up when they saw your writing actually would.

Reading

JUDGING THE EFFECTIVENESS OF AN AUTHOR'S DECISIONS

PURPOSE

Students are reminded to always approach reading informational texts with a critical eye.

LESSON INTENDED FOR

- Reading high-interest nonfiction
- Trade books
- Articles
- Textbooks
- Digital texts

MATERIALS NEEDED

- A space in the room, perhaps the classroom library or a meeting area, with baskets or stacks of nonfiction books available for perusing
- Students' independent reading books
- "Writers Consider Their Audiences as They Finish Their Pieces" chart (see page 185)

Lesson steps

1. Explain that they are toward the end of their reading of informational books.

2. Remind them that as writers, they tried to be very aware of what their readers need.

3. Recommend that as readers, now and in the future, they pick up all informational texts with a critical eye.

4. Share some tips for having a critical eye.

5. Ask them to test out those tips with the nearby texts.

What I Say to Students

You all have noticed that there are books all around us. They are here to remind us that we are readers, expert readers, who have read tons and tons of informational texts in the past several weeks. After today, we will be moving on to focus on new things, but I want to talk about one more thing before we go.

[Point to the chart, "Writers Consider Their Audiences as They Finish Their Pieces."]

Remember when we talked as writers about how important our audiences are and how we need to make changes to our writing to attract and keep them? Well, guess what? We are also the audience. And part of being an audience member is being a responsible one.

To be a responsible reader is to be a critical one. I want to you to leave here remembering that being a critical reader is a good thing to be. It means that you read looking for truth and quality. It means you will be a lifelong reader because you will go out of your way to read the texts that you enjoy and learn from. When more readers are critical, writers respond to that and create better material. When we read better material, we write better pieces.

I want to give you a few tips for being a critical reader.

First, critical readers look for what engages them. The best texts not only need to catch a reader's eye but also to hold the reader's attention throughout.

Secondly, critical readers read with the lens of truth. We make sure all of the facts are true and that even creative things are speaking the truth and are not needlessly slanted toward one perspective or another.

Third, critical readers read with a focus on craft. We look at word choice, organization, and sentence structure. We notice the extra effort that authors put into their writing to make it as strong as possible.

Before you leave this meeting today, I'd like you to grab a book or an article—or a few. You can do this by yourself or in the company of others. Then, I would like you to try out your critical eye. See what there is to see. What do you like and admire? What might you have a quibble with? Share what you are seeing with other readers around you, and discuss how what you are noticing might affect your next choices in reading materials.

Students examine their texts with a critical eye.

Writing

OPENING AND MAINTAINING A CONVERSATION WITH AUDIENCES

PURPOSE

Students learn techniques that help them achieve an inviting, conversational tone.

LESSON INTENDED FOR

- Personal expertise digital writing
- Content-specific digital writing
- Blog writing

MATERIALS NEEDED

- A demonstration text
- A list of ways digital writers can interact with readers (optional)
- A whiteboard or other record for brainstorming

Lesson steps

1. Ask students to consider some of the ways that reading online is different from reading a text in a printed book or magazine.

2. Discuss how one main difference is that online writers expect to have a relationship with their readers and actively cultivate that relationship.

3. Explain that the concept of digital literacy is not just about being able to read and write digitally but also about the ability to interact constructively with others online.

4. Give a few examples of ways that writers might interact with their audiences, recording on a chart or whiteboard as needed.

5. Ask students to help decide how the demonstration text could involve readers more.

6. Tuck in some teaching about responding to readers' interactions.

7. Encourage students to think of ways they could do similar work with their writing.

 ## What I Say to Students

You know, we've been talking about all of the ways that our reading and writing can change when we are dealing with online pieces. I'd like you to discuss this with some folks around you. What are some of the biggest differences between writing something for an online audience and writing something for a brick-and-mortar library or another type of publication where you may never hear from the reader?

[Listen in as students discuss.]

A few of you mentioned that one of the biggest differences, which we haven't really talked about yet, is that often when informational writers write something online, they do so knowing that their readers are going to respond to them. It's sort of expected. Part of what makes digital writing so interesting is that the wall between writer and reader is thinner. It's not as if the reader has no way to get in touch with the writer and the other way around.

This conversation between readers and writers exists with every style of writing, but it is a lot easier to make that connection when you are writing online. And since readers expect it, digital writers can do some purposeful work to get more involvement from their readers.

Let's think about some easy ways to get readers interested by interacting with online writing. Here's a list we can add to if you think something's missing.

- End the piece asking a question.

- Include a survey for readers to take.

- Suggest that readers share the piece with friends.

- Ask for readers to share their comments in a comments section.

- Respond to comments right away to encourage other readers to comment.

- Post photographs, videos, or other content that makes readers want to respond.

At this point, you know my rat piece pretty well. I'd like your input on this. What could I do to engage in conversation with readers and also get more readers to read the piece? **Think it over with someone sitting near you, and then, we'll do a little group brainstorming list.**

[Give students a few minutes to discuss this, and then, call them back together.]

Let's record some of your ideas.

- Create a survey of people's opinions about rats.

- Create a quiz to test people's rat knowledge at the beginning of the article so that they'll want to read more.

- Ask an opinion question at the beginning of the piece, and then, ask at the end if the piece changed the reader's mind. Ask something like, "Do you think rats are awful or incredible?"

- Once people start sharing their opinions about this question, make sure to respond to each one.

All of these are such great ideas! I also think it's important to note that if I do manage to get readers talking about my article, I need to try to keep the same voice and style as the piece I originally wrote. For instance, in my case, there's a definite leaning to rats being misunderstood, so when I respond to people, I would keep that opinion. I also have a lighthearted tone throughout, so I would want to keep that, too. And when we are engaging in a conversation with our readers, it's important to be respectful to them, both because it's the right thing to do and to help further the conversation. The more we engage with our readers, the more they'll understand what we were trying to say and perhaps the more new readers we will find, too.

So now it's your turn, digital writers! Today, when you are off working on your final touches for your piece, I want you to set aside a few minutes to think about ways to engage with your readers and perhaps get your information out to even more people!

Students work on achieving an inviting, conversational tone.

Reading

RESPONDING DIGITALLY TO THE TEXTS TO DEEPEN UNDERSTANDING

Lesson steps

1. Discuss that just as students tried to engage their readers when they worked on their writing pieces, the authors of the texts they read are trying to engage them.

2. Explain that readers can respond to texts in a variety of ways.

3. Delve into several digital options, using the chart.

4. Read aloud a text that students also have access to.

5. Ask students to work with partners or groups to try a few different ways to respond to that text digitally. For classes that need more guidance, assign groups and set up predesigned centers where each area has a set type of response and apps already bookmarked for student use.

6. Have students reflect on what worked and what they might want to try next time.

What I Say to Students

Earlier, we looked at some of the different ways that digital writers try to get their readers more engaged and to start a conversation with their readers. Now we're going to be looking at that same question from the other side of the desk. We're going to be considering some of the ways that we can respond to the texts that we're reading.

For example, we already know from all of our years of reading that we can always talk about a text. We know we can create art about a text. We know we can write letters to the authors. We can write sticky notes or marginal notes to record thoughts and questions. We can create graphic organizers to keep track of our thoughts and ideas. The list goes on. However, these are not

PURPOSE

Students explore a variety of ways to use digital tools to deepen their connection and comprehension.

LESSON INTENDED FOR

- Reading websites
- Reading blogs
- Reading other online content with multimodal features
- Reading analogue texts, responding digitally

MATERIALS NEEDED

- A few sample responses to share with students
- A chart of response options and apps, with the ability for students to add on (see page 192)
- A short class read-aloud with digital access for students (in this lesson, I use "Baby Talk Helps Infants Learn Language")
- A landing spot for recommended apps or response options on your classroom server, webpage, or other options

the only ways. And since we have been doing so much work lately as digital readers and writers, it seems to me that you are ready to explore ways that digital tools might offer you additional ways to respond to your texts. Let's go over a few options you might consider.

[Display the chart and read through it, discussing each idea. You can download the chart from the companion website.]

online resources

Available for download at **resources.corwin.com/ writersreadbetter**

Ways to respond to a text	Reasons to respond that way	Digital apps or platforms to try	Audience for this response
Annotate the text.	- The text is rich with details. - You are preparing for a book talk. - You are preparing to write about the text.	- iAnnotate - Show Me - Doctopus - Diig	- Self - Partner or club - Teacher
Write a review.	- You have strong feelings about the text. - You want others to know about the text.	- Social media (See Saw) - Library or bookstore site - In comments section (if available)	- Other readers - The author
Create a book or article trailer.	- You want to get other people to read the text. - You enjoyed the topic.	- iMovie - Flip Grid	- Other readers - The teacher
Write to the author.	- You had a strong reaction to the text. - You have unanswered questions or theories. - You want to communicate to the author.	- Visit the author's website - E-mail author - Comment on page the piece is posted on	- The author
Use a graphic organizer.	- You want to organize information from the text. - You want to share details and ideas with other readers. - You are preparing to present information from this text to a larger audience.	- Mindmeister - Prezi - Inspiration - Popplet - Mindomo	- Self - Partners or clubs - Teacher

Of course, there are other ways to respond to texts, but these are a few you might have thought about or heard about before. You can always add more. Today, we will look at a text together and then try out some different digital responses.

First, I will read aloud a multimodal article to you, so there will be some video and other links to explore as well. Then, I'm going to ask you to find one or two people who are interested in exploring a couple of different ways to respond to the text. You can use this chart to pick the ways that match your reasons for responding and the apps or platforms that look the most interesting to you.

[Read aloud the article, and then, give small groups about thirty minutes to explore their options. Then, call them back together and reflect.]

You may want to add a column to our chart for examples. As you continue to work on your own, please feel free to share some of your favorite experiments with the different digital response methods.

Students consider using digital tools to deepen their connection and comprehension.

PUBLISHER'S ACKNOWLEDGMENTS

Lynn M. Angus, K–12 English Language Arts Coordinator, DeKalb County School District, Stone Mountain, GA.

Helen S. Comba, Retired Supervisor of English Language Arts, The School District of the Chathams, Chatham, NJ.

Michael Rafferty, Director of Teaching and Learning, Region 14 Schools, Woodbury, CT.

Judy Wallis, Literacy Consultant, Sugar Land, TX.

RESOURCES

General Interest Children's and Young Adult Literature

online resources

Available for download at
**resources.corwin.com/
writersreadbetter**

Poop Happened!: A History of the World From the Bottom Up (2010) by Sarah Albee

Bugged: How Insects Changed History (2014) by Sarah Albee and Robert Leighton

An Egg Is Quiet (2014) by Dianna Hutts Aston

Fred Korematsu Speaks Up (2017) by Laura Atkins and Stan Yogi

That's Gross: Icky Facts That Will Test Your Gross-Out Factor (2012) by Crispin Boyer

How They Choked: Failures, Flops, and Flaws of the Awfully Famous (2016) by Georgia Bragg

Grand Canyon (2017) by Jason Chin

Disgusting History: The Smelliest, Dirtiest Eras of the Past 10,000 Years (2014) by James Corrick

A Black Hole Is Not a Hole (2017) by Carolyn Cinami DeCristafano

The Ultimate Body-Pedia: An Amazing Inside-Out Tour of the Human Body (2015) by Patricia Daniels and Christina Wildson

How to Make a Universe With 92 Ingredients: An Electrifying Guide to the Elements (2013) by Adrian Dingle

How to Swallow a Pig: Step-By-Step Advice From the Animal Kingdom (2015) by Steve Jenkins

The Story of Salt (2014) by Mark Kurlansky

Little Explorers: My Amazing Body (2015) by Ruth Martin and Allan Sanders

Two Truths and a Lie (2017) by Ammi-Joan Paquette and Laurie Ann Thompson

Tricky Vic: The Impossibly True Story of the Man Who Sold the Eiffel Tower (2015) by Greg Pizzoli

The Dreadful Smelly Colonies: The Disgusting Details About Life in Colonial America (2011) by Elizabeth Raum

Mesmerized: How Ben Franklin Solved a Mystery That Baffled All of France (2017) by Mara Rockliff

Vulture View (2007) by April Pulley Sayre

When Is a Planet Not a Planet? The Story of Pluto (2007) by Elaine Scott

Animals Nobody Loves (2002) by Seymour Simon

Stars (2006) by Seymour Simon

Can an Aardvark Bark? (2017) by Melissa Stewart

How Does a Bone Become a Fossil? (2016) by Melissa Stewart

No Monkeys, No Chocolate (2013) by Melissa Stewart

Inside Earthquakes (2011) by Melissa Stewart

Robots (2014) by Melissa Stewart

Pluto's Secret: An Icy World's Tale of Discovery (2015) by Margaret Weitekamp

Human Body Theater: A Nonfiction Revue (2015) by Maris Wicks

Topic-Specific Children's and Young Adult Literature

Big Cats

Big Cats: In Search of Lions, Leopards, Cheetahs, and Tigers (2012) by Steve Bloom

National Geographic Kids Everything Big Cats: Pictures to Purr About and Info to Make You Roar! (2011) by Elizabeth Carney

Cheetahs (2011) by Laura Marsh

Chasing Cheetahs: The Race to Save Africa's Fastest Cat (2017) by Sy Montgomery

Big Cats (1994) by Seymour Simon

Roald Dahl and World War II

Roald Dahl's Revolting Recipes (1997) by Roald Dahl

Boy: Tales of Childhood (2009) by Roald Dahl

Going Solo (2009) by Roald Dahl

The War in the Air: The Royal Air Force in World War II (1969)
by Gavin Lyall

Rats

Rats!: The Good, the Bad, and the Ugly by Richard Conniff

Oh Rats!: The Story of Rats and People (2006) by Albert Marrin

Rats: Observations on the History and Habitat of the City's Most Unwanted Inhabitants (2005) by Robert Sullivan

Misunderstood: Why the Humble Rat May Be Your Best Pet Ever (2016)
by Rachel Toor

What's Awake? Rats (2010) by Patricia Whitehouse

Buildings and Architecture

Cool Architecture: Filled With Fantastic Facts for Kids of All Ages (2015)
by Simon Armstrong

The Story of Buildings: From the Pyramids to the Sydney Opera House and Beyond (2014) by Patrick Dillon

Amazing Buildings (2003) by Kate Hayden

Building Big (2004) by David Macaulay

Cathedral (1981) by David Macaulay

Digital Resources

"Baby Talk Helps Infants Learn Language" from CNN: http://www.cnn
.com/2016/12/06/health/why-baby-talk-is-good/index.html

"Pavlof Volcano in Alaska still erupting, sending ash plume up to 37,000
feet" from CNN: http://www.cnn.com/2016/03/28/us/pavlof-volcano-
eruption-alaska/index.html

Time for Kids 5–6: https://www.timeforkids.com/g56/

National Geographic for Kids: https://kids.nationalgeographic.com/

Smithsonian Education Students: http://www.smithsonianeducation.org/students/

American Museum of Natural History Explore: https://www.amnh.org/explore

"Jennifer Anniston Did WHAT To Her Hair?" (false news) Stylecaster: http://stylecaster.com/beauty/jennifer-aniston-makeover/

All About Explorers (teacher-created false resources): https://www.allaboutexplorers.com/

"Building a Home" Plimoth Plantation: http://plimoth.org/learn/just-kids/homework-help/building-home#pilgrim%20houses

"Why We Laugh" Sophie Scott, video Ted2015: https://www.ted.com/talks/sophie_scott_why_we_laugh

"Does Laughing Help You Live Longer?" Wonderopolis: https://wonderopolis.org/wonder/does-laughing-help-you-live-longer

"Staring Contest/Discover the Forest" Ad Council Video: https://www.youtube.com/watch?v=ARLRv4XvzMQ

"#IAmAWitness" Animated Video: https://www.youtube.com/watch?v=V32xhSMhCXE

"Bill Nye the Science Guy Energy" Video: https://www.youtube.com/watch?v=8qmSzMwTkpk

"Earth" by Disneynature: to purchase or get more information about the video: http://nature.disney.com/earth

American Kennel Club: http://www.akc.org/dog-breeds/american-staffordshire-terrier/detail/

"Troublemakers" by Malcolm Gladwell, *The New Yorker:* https://www.newyorker.com/magazine/2006/02/06/troublemakers-2

"How did pit bulls get such a bad rap?" by Jon Bastian: https://www.cesarsway.com/about-dogs/pit-bulls/how-did-pit-bulls-get-a-bad-rap

"Meet the American Staffordshire Terrier" American Kennel Club: http://www.akc.org/dog-breeds/american-staffordshire-terrier/detail/

"Rats" – a sample set of digital examples of an excerpt from teacher demo writing https://padlet.com/mcolleencruz/rats

"Discover the Forest," Ad Council: https://www.youtube.com/watch?v=ARLRv4XvzMQ

"Stars," National Geographic: http://science.nationalgeographic.com/science/space/universe/stars-article/

"Cesar's Way," Cesar Milan: https://www.cesarsway.com/about-dogs/pit-bulls/how-did-pit-bulls-get-a-bad-rap

"All About Explorers": https://allaboutexplorers.com/

Plimoth Plantation: www.plimoth.org/learn/just-kids/homework-help/building-home#Pilgrim%20houses

REFERENCES

Allington, R. (2012). *What really matters for struggling readers: Designing research-based programs* (3rd ed.). New York, NY: Pearson.

Atwell, N. (2014). *In the middle: A lifetime of learning about writing, reading and adolescents* (3rd ed.). Portsmouth, NH: Heinemann.

Bomer, K. (2010). *Hidden gems: Naming and teaching from the brilliance of every student's writing.* Portsmouth, NH: Heinemann.

Bonyadi, A., & Zeinalpur, S. (2014, May). Perceptions of students towards self-selected and teacher-assigned topics in EFL writing. *Procedia – Social and Behavioral Sciences, 98,* 385–391.

Bonzo, J. D. (2008). To assign a topic or not: Observing fluency and complexity in intermediate foreign language writing. *Foreign Language Annals, 41*(4), 722–735.

Burns, P. C., Roe, B. D., & Ross, E. P. (1992). *Teaching reading in today's elementary schools* (5th ed.). Boston, MA: Houghton Mifflin.

Calkins, L. M. (1983). *Lessons from a child: On the teaching and learning of writing.* Portsmouth, NH: Heinemann.

Calkins, L. M. (1994). *The art of teaching writing.* Portsmouth, NH: Heinemann.

Calkins, L. M. (2000). *The art of teaching reading.* New York: Pearson

Calkins, L. (2013). *Units of study for teaching writing.* Portsmouth, NH: Heinemann.

Calkins, L. (2015). *Units of study for teaching reading.* Portsmouth, NH: Heinemann.

Chew. (1985). Instruction can link reading and writing. In J. Hansen, T. Newkirk, & D. Graves (Eds.), *Breaking ground: Teachers relate reading and writing in the elementary classroom.* Portsmouth, NH: Heinemann.

Clay, M. (1991). *Becoming literate: The construction of inner control.* Portsmouth, NH: Heinemann.

Clay, M. (2010). *Concepts about print.* Portsmouth, NH: Heinemann.

Eickholdt, L. (2015). *Learning from classmates: Using students' writing as mentor texts.* Portsmouth, NH: Heinemann.

Fletcher, R., & Portalupi, J. (2007). *Craft lessons.* Portland, ME: Stenhouse.

Fountas, I., & Pinnell, G. (2001). *Guiding readers and writers: Teaching comprehension, genre and content literacy.* Portsmouth, NH: Heinemann.

Gentry, J. R., & Peha, S. (2013). 5 ways to motivate young writers and readers. *Psychology Today.* Retrieved from www.psychologytoday.com/blog/raising-readers-writers-and-spellers/201310/5-ways-motivate-young-writers-and-readers

Gladwell, M. (2000). *The tipping point: How little things can make a big difference.* New York, NY: Little, Brown.

Gladwell, M. (2005). *Blink.* New York, NY: Little, Brown.

Graham, S., & Hebert, M. A. (2010). *Writing to read: Evidence for how writing can improve reading. A Carnegie Corporation Time to Act Report.* Washington, DC:

Alliance for Excellent Education. Retrieved from www.carnegie.org/media/filer_
   public/9d/e2/9de20604-a055-42da-bc00-77da949b29d7/ccny_report_2010_
   writing.pdf.

Graves, D. (1983). *Writing: Teachers & children at work*. Portsmouth, NH:
   Heinemann.

Graves, D. (1994). *A fresh look at writing*. Portsmouth, NH: Heinemann.

Harvey, S. (1998). *Nonfiction matters: Reading, writing and research in grades 3–8*.
   Portland, ME: Stenhouse.

Harvey, S., & Goudvis, A. (2017). *Strategies that work* (3rd ed.). Portland, ME:
   Stenhouse.

Hornsby, D., Sukarna, D., & Parry, J. (1988). *Read on: A conference approach to
   reading*. Portsmouth, NH: Heinemann.

Kohn, A. (1993). *Punished by rewards: The trouble with gold stars, incentive plans, A's,
   praise and other bribes*. Boston, MA: Houghton Mifflin.

Murray, D. (2003). *A writer teaches writing*. Boston, MA: Heinle.

Murray, D. (2013). *The craft of revision* (5th ed.). Boston, MA: Wadsworth.

Portalupi, J., & Fletcher, R. (2001). *Nonfiction craft lessons*. Portland, ME: Stenhouse.

Ray, K. W. (1999). *Wondrous words: Writers and writing in the elementary classroom*.
   Urbana, IL: NCTE.

Wilde, S. (2007). *Spelling strategies and patterns*. Portsmouth, NH: Heinemann.

Wilde, S. (2012). *Funner grammar: Fresh ways to teach usage, language, & writing
   conventions*. Portsmouth, NH: Heinemann.

INDEX

visual, 69

volume to signify importance,
105–106

weighing, to signal import, 101–106

Informational writing:

defining, 3

storytelling in, 107–109

structure and, 22–26

Inside Earthquakes (Stewart), 74–76

Internet:

fact-checking and, 82–83, 154–157

online reading, 188–190

See also Digital entries

Interpreting text, punctuation and,
177–178

Introductions:

reading, 150–151

writing, 145–149

Kidd, Diane, 74–76

Kurlansky, Mark, 11–12, 15–16, 55–56,
98–99, 171–173

Layall, Gavin, 68

Learning From Classmates 2015
(Eickholdt), 88

Lens of language, 120

Lens of truth, 187

Library, classroom, 45

Lift-the-flap book, 132–135

Literal comprehension:

drafting with placeholders, 57–58

noting facts, 59–60

quotation marks, 63–64

Little Explorers: My Amazing Body
(Martin), 132

Logical structure, table of contents and,
30–31

Main idea:

facts and, 111, 125–127

introductions and conclusions,
145–149

solutions at a glance, xi

titles and subtitles, meaning and,
167–168

Maps, as text features, 158

Marking text, 19

Marrin, Albert, 15–17, 27–29, 63–64

Martin, Ruth, 132

Meaning:

punctuation and, 177–178

spelling and, 179–181

structure, choice and, 27–29

titles and subtitles convey, 167–168

Mentor texts:

about, xxvi

Bears (Carney), 78–79

Boy (Dahl), 68

Craft Lessons (Fletcher), 87

Dear Zoo (Campbell), 119–121

Disgusting History (Corrick & Forest),
105–106

*Dreadful Smelly Colonies: The Disgusting
Details About Life in Colonial
America* (Raum), 128–130

Going Solo (Dahl), 68

Hidden Gems (Bomer), 88

*Impossible True Story of Tricky Vic:
The Man Who Sold the Eiffel
Tower* (Pizzoli), 59–60

Inside Earthquakes (Stewart), 74–76

Learning From Classmates
(Eickholdt), 88

Little Explorers: My Amazing Body
(Martin), 132

No Monkeys, No Chocolate (Stewart),
59–60

Oh Rats! (Marrin), 63–64

Pluto's Secret (Weitekamp & Kidd),
74–76

Roald Dahl's Revolting Recipes (Dahl),
68–69

Robots (Stewart), 46–47, 78–79

Scrapes With Snakes (Barr), 110–112

Story of Salt, The (Kurlansky), 55–56,
98–99, 171–173

Strategies that Work (Harvey &
Goudvis), 87

That's Gross (Boyer), 74

Thunderstorms (Stiefel), 116–118, 122–124

Ultimate Bodypedia, The (Daniels &
Wilsdon), 132

Units of Study for Writing or *Units of
Study for Reading* (Calkins), 87

Volcanoes (Schreiber), 78–79

War in the Air, The (Lyall), 68

*When is a Planet Not a Planet? The
Story of Pluto* (Scott), 74–76

See also Resources

Read-aloud texts:
    guide to, xxviii
    importance, xxx
Reader interactions, online reading,
    188–190
Reading:
    bias and, 128–130
    comprehension, digital tools, xxxi
    critical eye for, 186–187
    digital, xxxi, 38–41, 137–140
    drafting and, 43
    information stacking and, 54–56
    narrative, informational v., 110–112
    preparing for, text guide, xxvii–xxviii
    rereading for clues, 150–151
    series, 78–80
    vocabulary and, 122–124
Reading logs, 45
Reading plan, 139
Reliability, sources, 154–157
Reordering information, 94–97
Rereading, 19, 150–151
Research:
    drafting break to perform, 61–62
    jots to note facts, 59–60
    online, 68
    placeholders, drafting and, 57–58
Resource chart, 153
Resources:
    digital, 197–199
    general interest children and YA
        literature, 195–196
    topic specific YA literature, 196–197
    See also Mentor texts
Responding to texts:
    digitally, for understanding, 191–193
    lesson guide, xiii
    online engagement, 189–190
Response options chart, 192
Reviews, writing, 192t
Revision:
    facts and, 125–127
    introductions and conclusions, 148, 149
    multimodal texts, 132–135
    oral, 119–121
    placement of information, order,
        98–99
    storytelling and, 107–109
    table of contents, 103–104
    titles, subtitles and, 167–168

weighing information for importance,
    101–104
what to revise?, 89–90
Roald Dahl's Revolting Recipes (Dahl),
    68–69
Robots (Stewart), 46–49, 78–79
Root words, 179, 182

Scaffolding:
    accessibility, xxxii
    individual students, xxiv
    reading and writing lessons, xxi–xxii
Scheduling and timing, xxix–xxx
Schreiber, Ann, 78–79
Scott, Elaine, 74–76
Scott, Sophie, 65
Scrapes With Snakes (Barr), 110–112
Sections, structure within (video), x,
    50–53
Sell-checking, 179
Sentences:
paragraphs and, 170
punctuation tools, 174–176
Sequencing, 114–115
Series, reading, 78–80
Shocking facts, 125
Slide shows, 132, 133
Small-groups, xxiv
Smithsonian, The (website), xxxi
Social media shares, 138
Software, word-processing, xxxi
Solutions at a Glance, xi
"Some Reasons Informational Writers
    Include Stories in Their Pieces"
    chart, 108
"Some Strategies for Spotting Source
    Reliability" chart, 84–85
"Some Ways to Organize Information
    While Drafting Nonfiction Texts"
    chart, 51
Sources:
    evaluating nonfiction, 6–8
    identify, examine reliability,
        154–157
    quoting, describing or summarizing,
        152–153
    reliability of, 84–85
Speech-to-text software, xxiv
Spell-check, 182
Spelling, meaning and, 179–181

CORWIN A SAGE Publishing Company

Helping educators make the greatest impact

CORWIN HAS ONE MISSION: to enhance education through intentional professional learning.

We build long-term relationships with our authors, educators, clients, and associations who partner with us to develop and continuously improve the best evidence-based practices that establish and support lifelong learning.

BECAUSE ALL TEACHERS ARE LEADERS

Nancy Frey, John Hattie, and Douglas Fisher

Imagine students who understand their educational goals and monitor their progress. This illuminating book focuses on self-assessment as a springboard for markedly higher levels of student achievement.

Dave Stuart Jr.

Streamline your instructional practice so that you're teaching smarter, not harder, and kids are learning, doing, and flourishing in ELA and content-area classrooms.

Berit Gordon

Discover how to transform your classroom into a vibrant reading environment. This groundbreaking book combines the benefits of classic literature with the motivational power of choice reading.

Patty McGee

Patty McGee helps you transform student writers by showing you what to do to build tone, trust, motivation, and choice into your daily lessons, conferences, and revision suggestions.

Leslie Blauman

Teaching Evidence-Based Writing: Fiction and *Nonfiction* help you educate students on how to do their best analytical writing about fiction and nonfiction. Whether annotating a text or writing a paragraph, an essay, or response on a test, your students will know how to support their thinking.

Gravity Goldberg and Renee Houser

With *What Do I Teach Readers Tomorrow? Fiction* and *Nonfiction*, discover how to move your readers forward with in-class, actionable formative assessment in just minutes a day with a proven 4-step process and lots of next-step resources.

800-233-9936